They Also Serve

Rosemary Greenlaw

Copyright © 2015 Rosemary Greenlaw

All rights reserved.

ISBN: 978-1517327132

The story of
the PDSA's Dickin Medal,
and of the brave and faithful
animals who received it
1943-2015

CONTENTS

1	THEY ALSO SERVE	1
2	A FOREIGN FIELD	5
3	JUDY'S STORY	19
4	THE HOME FRONT	25
5	SHEILA'S STORY	35
6	THE FLYING SQUAD	39
7	SIMON'S STORY	57
8	AND STILL THEY SERVE	63
9	SALTY & ROSELLE'S STORIES	77
10	LEST WE FORGET	83
	WARRIOR'S STORY	84
	Appendix 1: Roll of Honour	88
	Appendix 2: Further Reading	98

"They Had No Choice"
*– inscription on the Animals in War Memorial,
Hyde Park, London*

Chapter 1
THEY ALSO SERVE

The Dickin Medal is widely recognised as "the animals' Victoria Cross", the highest award for exceptional bravery and devotion to duty on active service. Instituted in 1943, it has to date (2015) been awarded only sixty-five times. These sixty-five creatures – 32 pigeons, 29 dogs, three horses and one cat – may be the bravest of the brave, but they also stand as representatives of all the hundreds of thousands of their comrades who went to war alongside the armed forces and Civil Defence units, and who suffered and died with them. Their stories are truly remarkable.

The sacrifice and loyalty of the animal kingdom in the service of man's wars is enormous.

The Dickin Medal is a large, bronze medallion bearing, within a laurel wreath, the words 'For Gallantry' and 'We Also Serve'. The ribbon is striped in green, dark brown and pale blue, representing water, earth and air to symbolise the three branches of the armed services. The recipient's name and details are inscribed on the reverse.

The Medal is awarded by the PDSA (the People's Dispensary for Sick Animals) and its history is intimately bound up with that of the PDSA and its remarkable founder, Maria Dickin.

Maria Dickin

Maria Elisabeth Dickin, the eldest of eight children of a Free Church Minister, was born in London in 1870. Mia, as she was known, grew up into a bright, confident, independent and articulate young woman; against the conventions of the time, which decreed that well-brought-up girls of her class did not go out to work, she opened a voice-production studio in Wimpole Street which quickly attracted a string of well-known clients. When she was 28 she married her cousin, Arnold Dickin, a successful chartered accountant, and finally gave up the world of work to settle into the role of society wife and hostess. Her salons and dinner parties glittered with prominent people from politics, commerce and the law; she appeared to have everything a young matron of her age could desire. But giving up her career had left this dynamic, industrious young woman bored and restless.

She took up social work – a socially acceptable activity for a respectable woman in that day and age – and threw herself into it with her customary dedication. Her work took her into the homes of the desperately poor in London's East End, and in those homes, and in the crowded, filthy streets, she found the cause which was to define her life.

The PDSA

Starving dogs and cats, with ghastly mange and running sores, scavenged in the dirt for anything they could eat; rabbits, goats and chickens eked out miserable lives in grim little backyards; working horses and donkeys lived in appalling conditions and worked long hours pulling overloaded carts, their ill-fitting harness rubbing galls in their skin.

In her book *The Cry of the Animal* Maria said 'The suffering and misery of these poor, uncared-for creatures in our overcrowded areas was a revelation to me. I had no idea it existed, and it made me indescribably miserable.' She was fired by a determination to do something about the situation. The question was, what? The RSPCA (Royal Society for the Prevention of Cruelty to Animals), founded in 1822, worked against cruelty and neglect; but when her own much-loved Yorkshire terrier fell ill and had to be put humanely to sleep, it dawned on Maria that for the poor who could not afford the cost of veterinary treatment, and for their animals, there was nowhere to turn. She began to think about setting up a clinic and dispensary to provide medicines and advice.

Finding suitable premises, and securing the necessary funding, was no easy task, and it seemed that she met resistance at every turn. A less determined woman would have surrendered to despair; Maria soldiered on and finally, on Saturday 17th November 1917, the first 'People's Dispensary for Sick Animals of the Poor' opened in a cellar in Whitechapel. A sign outside read

Bring your sick animals.
Do not let them suffer.
All animals treated.
All treatment free.

The response was overwhelming; so big were the crowds bringing their animals for treatment the police had to be called to restore order. They were soon treating over a hundred animals a day, and had to move to larger premises.

Jubilant, Maria said 'I must have dispensaries throughout the whole of the East of London... no, throughout the whole of London... throughout England – then the British Isles, the British Empire!' In 1921, in a converted horse-drawn caravan, she travelled with a veterinary surgeon throughout Britain, treating animals and setting up clinics. Within two years there were 16 dispensaries in Britain, as well as a motor-caravan dispensary, and one in Tangiers. From there things really took off. The Animal's Sanatorium, the first in Europe, opened at Ilford in London in 1928; by 1935 there were five PDSA hospitals, 71 dispensaries, eleven motorised mobile dispensaries, and dispensaries in Egypt and Greece; within the next two years dispensaries opened in South Africa and Palestine.

The Dickin Medal

The Second World War (1939-45) was a busy and difficult time for the PDSA. The mobile dispensaries were put on standby in the large cities to help the large numbers of animals injured, traumatised and rendered homeless by the bombing, and in addition Animal Rescue Squads were organised to rescue animals from the ruins. Despite being so busy with the rescue effort, Maria saw the courage and devotion to duty of the animals serving with the armed forces, and on the Home Front with the Civil Defence units. In 1943 she was instrumental in setting up the Allied Forces Mascot Club to obtain recognition for all the animals and birds that served their country during the war. Membership was confined to creatures serving with the Allied Forces (not necessarily British) and the Civil Defence services.

It met with great success and approval and there was a very large membership.

She also felt that these brave animals deserved recognition, and she was inspired to create a medal to be awarded in outstanding cases. Award of the Medal, which is specifically for animals in war, can only be considered on receipt of an official recommendation; it was awarded 54 times between 1943 and 1949. It quickly caught the imagination of the public, and many of the recipients became national heroes.

After a lapse of more than fifty years it was revived, and a further eleven medals have been awarded since 2000, as well as one honorary medal to pay tribute to all the animals who served with courage and devotion in the First World War. In addition to the Dickin Medal, the PDSA also award the Gold Medal ("the animals' George Cross"), instituted in 2002, for outstanding animal bravery and exceptional dedication in civilian life.

Ilford PDSA Animal Cemetery, established in the 1920s, is the final resting place of more than 3,000 animals, including 12 animal heroes from the Second World War that were awarded the Dickin Medal. The cemetery was refurbished in 2007 with a Lottery grant; graves were restored and new gravestones erected for some of the animal heroes.

Maria's Legacy

Maria devoted her life to suffering animals, and was awarded the OBE and the CBE in recognition of her work. She died in 1951, at the age of 81, but the PDSA has gone on, growing in both stature and reputation. The PDSA today provides two million free treatments every year in the UK, and while most of the overseas operations closed in the 1970s the PDSA South Africa and PDSA Cairo continue as independent operations, no longer part of the UK organisation.

Towards the end of her life Maria wrote, 'Today we are all thinking about what each of us can do towards making the world a better place for every man, woman and child to live in. We must not forget to include the animals in our programme, they too must have a better world to live in.' Thanks to her vision and humanity, and the untiring work of the organisation she founded, millions of sick and injured animals have indeed found that better world.

Chapter 2
A FOREIGN FIELD

For as long as man has waged war with man, dogs have accompanied him into the front line.

Military history is inseparable from images of the horse – the Scots Greys at Waterloo, the Charge of the Light Brigade in the Crimea, the artillery teams struggling in the mud of the Western Front in the First World War – but those days are now gone. Dogs, however, remain an integral part of the modern army. From ancient Egypt to the present day, they have been trained to attack, track, guard, patrol, carry messages, and to bring down infantry and even cavalry. The Romans deployed entire companies of fighting dogs, one company per legion. In the First World War they were employed by both sides to deliver messages and to carry light loads such as ammunition and first aid supplies to the front line, while the Belgians used large Bouviers des Flandres to haul light artillery.

Casualty or 'Mercy' dogs were trained to deliver first-aid to soldiers stuck in the mud of no-man's land. After heavy fighting, they were sent out into the field by their handlers in the Royal Army Medical Corps with supplies, such as stimulants and bandages, to give desperate men a chance to stabilise their wounds before medics could reach them, or so that they could make their own way back to British lines. Originally trained in the late 1800's by the Germans, these dogs were trained to find the wounded and dying on battlefields; soldiers who could help themselves to supplies would tend to their own wounds, whilst other more gravely wounded soldiers would seek the company of a Mercy dog to wait with them whilst they died.

When war broke out in 1914, there were no military dogs of any sort attached to the British Army save for one sole Airedale Terrier, who served with the 2nd Battalion Norfolk Regiment as a sentry and accompanied the battalion to France. Lt Col E.H. Richardson, however, was convinced of the essential role dogs could fill in wartime. He began to supply dogs for sentry and patrol work, finding that Airedales displayed the ideal combination of qualities. It was in response to a letter from an officer of the Royal Artillery in the winter of 1916, that Richardson turned his attention to training dogs specifically as messengers. The officer pointed out that trained dogs would be able to keep up communication between his outpost and the battery during a heavy bombardment, when noise and communication difficulties rendered telephones practically useless and when the risk to human runners was enormous. Richardson, after a number of experiments, successfully trained two Airedales to carry messages for two miles without a hitch and on New Year's Eve the two dogs, named Wolf and Prince, departed for France.

One of their first tasks was to carry a message four miles to brigade headquarters from the front line through a smoke barrage, a task completed within an hour. It soon became clear that dogs were faster, steadier, more nimble across shell holes and muddy terrain, and more difficult to spot than human messengers. The two dogs were trailblazers. With Wolf and Prince having proved the usefulness of dogs at the front, demand for more messenger dogs grew and Lt Col Richardson was asked by the War Office to establish his British War Dog School in 1917.

Dogs for the school came from dogs' homes, and police around the country were instructed to send any strays, of all breeds, to the school. When even this was not sufficient, the War Office appealed to the public via notices in the Press to donate their own pets, with the promise that, at a time when food shortages were beginning to be felt, the dog would be well fed and cared for in the Army.

The response was excellent and many family pets were soon doing their bit for King and Country, though many of the letters accompanying the donated dogs were heart-rending. One little girl wrote, 'We have let Daddy go to fight the Kaiser, and now we are sending Jack to do his bit.' A lady wrote, 'I have given my husband and my sons, and now that he too is required, I give my dog.' Certain breeds were considered better suited to the task, particularly sheepdogs, collies, lurchers, Irish terriers, Welsh terriers, deerhounds and of course, Airedales. Fox terriers were considered too fond of play, retrievers were too compliant and unlikely to show an independence of thought while any dog with a 'gaily carried tail, which curled over its back or sideways,' was rarely of any value according to Richardson!

Messenger dogs were used in both the First and Second World Wars to carry messages in battle, and in the First World War dogs were used to lay communication cables, dashing across the battlefield spooling out cable from reels carried on their backs. Both messenger dogs and cable dogs were trained to respond to two handlers, so that they could be sent from one to the other.

One of the most famous messenger dogs was Rags, who served with the 1st Infantry Division (U.S.) during the First World War. Rags, a scruffy little terrier, saved many lives by delivering vital messages during the Meuse-Argonne offensive despite being bombed, gassed and partially blinded. Found as a stray puppy in Paris he was devoted to his 'men' and was recorded as leading medics to wounded men in the field through fog and gunfire. In the Second World War, a Russian dog sent to deliver a message during the battle of Stalingrad travelled for about 10 kilometres and was wounded nine times during the trip. Like the Roman dog battalions messenger dogs have now been consigned to history, having been overtaken by reliable communications technology.

At the outbreak of the Second World War the military planners were convinced that the dog, so prominent in the Great War of 1914-18, would have no place in modern, mechanised warfare. It soon emerged, however, that the Germans were using large numbers of specially-trained dogs, and gradually the view came to accepted in Britain that dogs had a valuable contribution to make. Once more, Lt Col Richardson went to bat, as he had done in the First World War, and in 1942 the War Dog School swung into action. Dogs were offered by the public, and the RSPCA and the Canine Defence League helped with recruitment rather than face the heartbreak of destroying thousands of healthy dogs made homeless by bombing, or by owners who could not feed them on restrictive rationing. By May 1944 some 7,000 dogs had passed through the training school, being trained for a variety of roles.

Guard dogs, or sentry dogs, were (and still are) used to defend troops and military installations, both at home and overseas. Ever vigilant, their keen senses of smell and hearing have provided countless thousands of serving troops with much-needed security, particularly at night. Dogs are an invaluable aid to ground troops in jungle warfare, over open country or in urban areas; their ability to detect intruders and their speed and agility in pursuit and apprehension make dogs a formidable deterrent to stealthy attack. Dogs have been used as 'scouts' since the Second World War, trained to quietly locate and indicate booby-traps, as well as snipers and other concealed enemies. The dogs' keen senses make them far more effective than humans at detecting these dangers. One handler and dog can cover an area that would otherwise require four or five foot patrols, and can do it more thoroughly.

In the modern age a new job has developed for dogs, as detection or sniffer dogs, trained to find explosives, arms and drugs. This work saves lives and defuses volatile situations in the military's peace-keeping role all over the world. Five of the six most recent British recipients of the Dickin Medal have been sniffer dogs, deployed in Iraq and Afghanistan, finding weapons, bombs and explosives.

The Russians, too, employed dogs – over 60,000 of them – during the Second World War. Bizarrely, they trained dogs to carry explosives underneath German tanks; they had a surprising rate of success. In one incident, at Glukhova, six dogs destroyed five enemy panzers within an hour; during the siege of Stalingrad, a squad of tank destroyer dogs destroyed thirteen tanks; at Kursk, sixteen dogs destroyed twelve tanks. Ultimately the plan was abandoned since the dogs didn't seem able to tell German tanks from Russian. On sleds during the winter or small carts in the summer, dogs brought ammunition to the battlefront, and took the wounded on their way back. Dogs rescued tens, possibly hundreds, of thousands of people from the battlefield. If a man was unconscious, the dog licked his face until he came to his senses. Russian messenger dogs delivered more than 20,000 messages and laid about 5,000 miles (8,000 km) of telephone wires where it was impossible for a soldier to pass.

Meanwhile, dogs also demonstrated an invaluable aptitude for detecting landmines. More than 300 large cities in Eastern Europe were cleared of mines with the help of dogs. Despite all these unexpected roles, however, nearly all modern military dogs fit into the roles of guard, sentry, patrol or scout dogs or detection and sniffer dogs.

All British military dogs, and their handlers, now come under the remit of the Royal Army Veterinary Corps, and are deployed with various units as and when required.

One of the finest, and simplest, tributes to the dogs that stand beside men in war comes from Tom Mitchell, an American serviceman who fought in Vietnam:

We lived with our best friends. He (or she) saved our lives many times. We shared our cookies, cakes and other goodies from home with our best friends. We read them our love letters, and yes, even the 'Dear Johns.' We told them what we wanted to do in 'The World.' They knew everything about us. When we were sick they would comfort us, and when we were injured they protected us. They didn't care how much money we had or what color our skin was. Heck, they didn't even care if we were good soldiers. They loved us unconditionally. And we loved them. Still do.

Dogs of all shapes and sizes served with British troops in action overseas during the Second World War. They served as guards, on patrol, as loyal companions and faithful friends. They fought, suffered and died alongside their comrades, and most of them live on only in the hearts of the men they served with. A few, by acts of conspicuous gallantry, gained wider recognition and are remembered on the roll of animals who have been awarded the Dickin Medal. Their stories are told here.

Bob – Mongrel
6th Royal West Kent Regt.
Date of Award: 24 March 1944
Citation: *"For constant devotion to duty with special mention of Patrol work at Green Hill, North Africa, while serving with the 6th Battalion Queens Own Royal West Kent Regt."*

The first dog to receive the Dickin Medal was Bob, a white mongrel, who was attached to an infantry unit in North Africa. One cold and rainy night he was sent out with his comrades on patrol. Suddenly Bob froze and, despite the encouragement and then the increasingly heated orders of his human comrades he flatly refused to advance. It was not until an unexpected noise betrayed the presence of an enemy unit that the men realised Bob had saved them from walking into a trap and being killed or captured. An NCO wrote to the Allied Forces Mascot Club that Bob 'did magnificent work throughout the whole North African campaign; running messages and doing patrol work. Many were saved by his timely warnings.' Bob subsequently participated in the Sicilian and Italian invasions.

Rob – Collie

War Dog No. 471/332 Special Air Service
Date of Award: 22 January 1945
Citation: *"Took part in landings during North African Campaign with an Infantry unit and later served with a Special Air Unit in Italy as patrol and guard on small detachments lying-up in enemy territory. His presence with these parties saved many of them from discovery and subsequent capture or destruction. Rob made over 20 parachute descents."*

Well, perhaps. Or perhaps not.

Incredibly, it appears that the story of 'Rob the SAS dog' was simply an elaborate hoax. Quentin 'Jimmy' Hughes, a former SAS training officer who was awarded the Military Cross and Bar for a raid and subsequent escape in Italy, revealed all in his autobiographical book about the SAS, *Who Cares Who Wins?*

Rob was popular in the regiment, and the particular favourite of quartermaster Tom Burt. When Rob's owners, who had lent him to the Army to help the war effort, decided they would like their dog back, the men devised a plan to keep him. The idea was to send him on a parachute jump, and Hughes would then write to Rob's owners to say that the dog's services were indispensable. It gets worse – they contrived a suitable parachute harness, enlisted the aid of the RAF and set off for the jump. Unfortunately quite a strong wind got up during the flight and the RAF decided it would be dangerous to drop Rob that day. Rob hadn't left the British Isles and hadn't made even a single parachute drop.

Still, Hughes decided to write the letter anyway. Rob had made repeated parachute drops, the letter said, in Italy and North Africa, and on the ground had saved many men by alerting them to danger. Hughes sent the letter off, and thought the matter would end there. To his horror, Rob's owners were so proud that they passed the letter on to the PDSA, who awarded the dog the Dickin Medal, and on 3rd February 1945 Rob was taken to London to receive the medal despite the fact that, according to one of the officers from his regiment, his war service had amounted to little more than wagging his tail and cheering up the men. Hughes said later, 'Nobody survived 20 parachute drops, let alone a dog. You were lucky to survive three.' Rob died in 1952.

All the people involved in this tale have since died, and it is probable that the truth will never now be established beyond doubt. But perhaps, if the story of the hoax is true, Rob deserves his medal anyway, for being such a good companion and morale-booster that the men around him were prepared to concoct such an elaborate charade to keep him with them.

And perhaps he can be regarded as holding the medal on behalf of all the regimental mascots, all the waifs and strays picked up by troops all over the world; all the loving animals whose contribution to the war effort was to provide servicemen in difficult and dangerous situations, far away from their homes and families, with love, companionship and, ultimately, the courage to carry on.

Rifleman Khan – Alsatian
6th Battalion Cameronians (Scottish Rifles)
Date of Award: 27 March 1945
Citation: *"For rescuing L/Cpl. Muldoon from drowning under heavy shell fire at the assault of Walcheren, November 1944, while serving with the 6th Cameronians (SR)."*

Rifleman Khan, a handsome Alsatian, was donated to the war effort by the Railton family of Surrey and, after training, saw action in Europe, being assigned to Corporal Muldoon of the 6th Battalion of the Cameronians. The two formed a comfortable bond and worked closely together.

In the autumn of 1944, with the war in Europe drawing to a close and much of southern Holland liberated, the Allies turned their attention to the German-occupied island of Walcheren. The island controlled the road to Antwerp, and its capture was vital.

The 6th Battalion of the Cameronians were detailed to assist the mainly Canadian forces in their drive to liberate Walcheren. The Germans were not prepared to give up the island easily and the Allied troops faced heavy fire, while bad weather hampered air cover. On the night of 1st–2nd November the battalion, including Muldoon and Rifleman Khan, embarked on assault craft packed with men and equipment to cross the Sloe channel, a dangerous crossing under heavy mortar and artillery fire. As they approached Walcheren the boat carrying Khan and Cpl Muldoon was hit, and men and equipment were flung into the water. Khan struck out for the shore and scrambled out onto the bank, vigorously shaking the water out of his coat, and began dashing up and down the shore looking for Muldoon. A non-swimmer, Muldoon could only splash helplessly, struggling to keep his head above the surface while artillery fire tore into the water around him. Suddenly he saw Khan ploughing through the water towards him. Khan had noticed his absence and come back for him. Through shellfire and oil slicks, the dog reached him, seized the shoulder of his tunic in his teeth and, turning for shore, battled his way back through the unceasing roar of shellfire. It was a long and arduous swim – the third of the night for Khan – but at last, the soldier clinging to the dog's coat, they reached safety. Walcheren Island was liberated, after heavy fighting, on 8th November.

At the end of the war Muldoon pleaded to be allowed to keep the dog, but in accordance with the original agreement Khan was returned to his owners. He seemed restless and unhappy, however, unable to settle back into civilian life.

In 1946 he was invited to participate in a War Dog parade, and the Railtons asked Muldoon to lead him in the parade. Their reunion was ecstatic, and the Railtons realised that the bond between them was unbreakable; generously they gave him up to his old army handler. Reunited with Cpl Muldoon, Rifleman Khan settled down into a happy retirement.

Rifleman Khan is believed to be buried in the animals' cemetery at Edinburgh Castle.

Judy - Pedigree Pointer
Date of Award: May 1946
Citation: *"For magnificent courage and endurance in Japanese prison camps, which helped to maintain morale among her fellow prisoners and also for saving many lives through her intelligence and watchfulness."*

Judy's story is told in Chapter 3.

Punch and Judy – Boxer dog and bitch
Date of Awards: November 1946
Citation: *"These dogs saved the lives of two British Officers in Israel by attacking an armed terrorist who was stealing upon them unawares and thus warning them of their danger. Punch sustained 4 bullet wounds and Judy a long graze down her back."*

On the evening of 5th August 1946 Lt Col A.H.K. Campbell and Lt Col H.G.G. Niven were relaxing at home in a Jerusalem suburb, with their boxer dogs Punch and Judy. The dogs suddenly became aware of intruders inside the compound. Racing into the darkness and barking furiously, they were met with a burst of sub-machine gun fire from the terrorist (or possibly two) who had broken through the barbed-wire perimeter of the compound. Apparently the intruders were stealthily creeping towards the house with the intention of killing the British officers. The barking and gunfire alerted the officers, thwarting the attack and thus saving their lives. A search of the compound revealed that Punch had been seriously wounded, having been hit by four bullets; and Judy, with a long graze down her back, was found guarding her brother. Nine expended rounds were later found in the garden. Both dogs made a full recovery from their wounds.

Judy's owner, Lt Col Niven, later served in Palestine as Adjutant General.

Ricky – Welsh Collie
Date of Award: 29 March 1947
Citation: *"This dog was engaged in cleaning the verges of the canal bank at Nederweert, Holland. He found all the mines but during the operation one of them exploded. Ricky was wounded in the head but remained calm and kept at work. Had he become excited he would have been a danger to the rest of the section working nearby."*

Ricky, a Welsh sheepdog, was loaned to the war effort at the beginning of the war. He was trained as a mine detector. The British were the first to use dogs for this work after the Germans introduced a non-metallic mine, which baffled the electronic mine detectors. These dogs, known as 'M-Dogs', were trained to sniff out buried mines and, when they located one, to lie down facing it, about five feet from it, and wait for their handler to deal with it. It was difficult and dangerous work, and the dogs chosen for it had to have special qualities: they had to be nimble and sure-footed, calm and disciplined, as well as possessing great intelligence.

After D-Day Ricky and his handler, Private Maurice Yelding, worked their way through France and Belgium and into Holland with the advancing Allied troops. On 3rd December 1944 he was attached to a squad clearing mines from the bank of the Nederweert canal bank; he successfully located three mines that day. Suddenly disaster struck; one of the mines exploded. The section commander was killed instantly and Ricky, injured, was thrown down the bank of the canal. He had shrapnel wounds to his head, narrowly missing his eyes. Struggling to his feet, Ricky remained calm and quiet; had he gone dashing madly round in a panic he may well have triggered other mines and endangered the rest of the squad. He continued calmly with his task despite his injuries, and indeed worked until the end of the war.

The Army was so impressed by his abilities they tried to buy him from his owner, but she insisted on having her pet returned to her.

Ricky died in 1953 and is buried at the Ilford Animal Cemetery.

Brian (Bing) – Alsatian

Date of Award: 29 March 1947

Citation: *"This patrol dog was attached to a Parachute Battalion of the 13th Battalion Airborne Division. He landed in Normandy with them and, having done the requisite number of jumps, became a fully-qualified Paratrooper."*

Brian (known in the Army as Bing) was a tough paratrooper. He trained hard for his deployment with the British Army. During his training, he learned how to identify minefields, and to protect his comrades-in-arms on the battlefield.

The 13th Parachute Battalion taught four patrol dogs, including Brian, to parachute from aeroplanes. Each dog had its own harness and static line parachute which opened automatically during descent. With the expectation of an edible reward, the dogs learned to jump immediately after their handlers. (In the 9th Parachute Battalion, dogs were taught to jump before their handlers.) Then came the day that the dogs had trained for, D-Day, 6th June 1944.

Everything seemed to be going according to plan until the hatch was opened. The planes were surrounded by bangs and whizzes, and loud salvos of flak threw yellow light onto the gray clouds. After the men had jumped, Brian turned around and holed up in the back of the aircraft. The jump master on board, who was responsible for coordinating the jump, was forced to unplug his radio equipment, catch the dog and toss him out of the plane. Poor Brian's jump didn't go as smoothly as his training jumps had; he was left hanging in the branches of the tree his parachute had got caught in. He then had to wait for two hours until his comrades found him, with two deep cuts in his face, most likely from German mortar fire.

In what followed, Brian and the other dogs proved to be very useful, especially for locating mines and booby traps. 'They would sniff excitedly over it for a few seconds and then sit down looking back at the handler with a quaint mixture of smugness and expectancy,' one soldier wrote, noting that the dogs would then be rewarded with a treat. 'The dogs also helped on patrols by sniffing out enemy positions and personnel, hence saving many Allied lives,' he added.

Brian was there when the Allies liberated Normandy. A few months before the war's end he parachuted into western Germany, from where he marched to the Baltic Sea.

Stuffed, he now resides in the Imperial War Museum at Duxford, Cambridgeshire.

Antis – Alsatian

Date of Award: 28 January 1949

Citation: *"Owned by a Czech airman, this dog served with him in the French Air Force and RAF from 1940 to 1945, both in N. Africa and England. Returning to Czechoslovakia after the war, he substantially helped his master's escape across the frontier when after the death of Jan Masaryk, he had to fly from the Communists."*

When Czech airman Vaclav Bozdech was shot down over France in 1940 he did two remarkable things: he rescued a tiny German Shepherd puppy from a bombed-out farmhouse and, tucking the puppy into his jacket, he made his way to freedom. Thus began an enduring partnership. Vaclav, who had fled Czechoslovakia when his homeland fell to the Nazis in 1939, flew with the French Air Force and then with the Royal Air Force in England, smuggling Antis into Britain to evade the quarantine laws. Antis lived with him on base, and when Vaclav and his crew went on bombing missions the dog would watch him depart and would be there to greet him on his return. There came an operation when Antis was not waiting to see his master off; Vaclav assumed he was in one of the huts. Some time into the flight, however, at 12,000 feet, he discovered Antis lying on the floor of the bomber, gasping for breath. Vaclav had to share his oxygen mask with him. It was a difficult mission, with several narrow escapes, and the crew decided Antis had brought them luck. From then on, the dog flew with them. On every mission he lay at Vaclav's feet in the gun turret. The turret of a bomber lumbering through the sky over enemy-held country is not the safest place to be, and Antis was wounded several times, never complaining but lying still and quiet, his wounds not discovered until the plane landed. It was, of course, strictly against regulations, but many a blind eye was turned until the secret could be kept no longer. For five years, from 1940 to 1945, Antis flew with his crew, always bounding out eagerly to the plane, undeterred by danger and injury; he flew on 32 missions in all.

Not content with an RAF career, Antis decided he had a role to play in Civil Defence as well. On an off-duty visit to Liverpool in September 1940, Vaclav and Antis were caught in an air-raid. Civil Defence wardens, seeing Antis, assumed he was a search-and-rescue dog and called on Vaclav to help them; Antis, with no training at all, found two people buried in a bombed house, thereby saving their lives, as well locating as two more who were beyond aid.

At the end of the war Vaclav returned to his native Czechoslovakia, and of course he took Antis with him. Sadly, for Vaclav, as for so many of his countrymen, the end of hostilities in 1945 did not signal a return to peaceful times. Czechoslovakia had fallen into the Soviet sphere of influence and something close to civil war was raging. Vaclav was on the 'wrong' side in this struggle, having fought for the West. In 1948 he had to flee from his homeland for a second time, leaving his wife and baby son behind, making his way to the US Occupied Zone in Germany and eventually to England. Throughout this dangerous overland journey Antis protected his master time and again. Back in Britain, Vaclav re-joined the RAF and served until 1961.

Antis's adventures encompassed not only the war but a turbulent and dangerous time after it. Like so many Czech and Polish flyers, Vaclav and Antis found eventual sanctuary in Britain, having played their part in defeating the German occupiers but being powerless against the forces rising against them in their own homelands. Antis received his Dickin Medal from Field Marshall Wavell in 1949.

In 1953 Vaclav was stationed in the north of Scotland. Antis, at 14, had been fading for some time; when it became clear he was dying Vaclav, at the request of the PDSA, travelled to London with him so that he could be put to sleep in Ilford and buried there. On his gravestone is written: 'Antis D.M. Alsatian, died 11th August 1953, aged 14 years.' Underneath are two inscriptions. The first reads:

> *There is an old belief*
> *That on some solemn shore*
> *Beyond the sphere of grief*
> *Dear friends shall meet once more*

The second, in Czech, reads simply *Verny Az Do Smrti*, which means 'Loyal Unto Death'.

Tich – Egyptian Mongrel
1st Battalion King's Royal Rifle Corps
Date of Award: 1 July 1949
Citation: *"For loyalty, courage and devotion to duty under hazardous conditions of war 1941 to 1945, while serving with the 1st King's Rifle Corps in North Africa and Italy."*

Tich was a mongrel, mostly terrier but with a noticeable dash of Dachshund. She was one of the countless starving strays who touched the hearts of British soldiers serving in North Africa. Tich pulled her 'I'm a pathetic little waif' act for the 1st Battalion

King's Royal Rifle Corps, and the troops adopted her as their mascot and showered her with titbits and cuddles. With an entire battalion of devoted masters and all the food she could eat, Tich had landed firmly on her little paws.

Under the care of Rifleman Thomas Walker, a medic, Tich went into action with the battalion across North Africa to El Alamein, riding on the Bren gun carrier or the stretcher jeep. Walker and Tich were usually in the thick of things, dashing out in their jeep to bring in casualties, often under a steady barrage of fire. One day she was wounded in the line of duty, sustaining a broken nose and severe lacerations from shrapnel. The unit's Medical Officer was pessimistic, but Thomas devotedly nursed his little Desert Rat back to health. She served with the battalion for five years, through North Africa and Italy. When the Allies invaded Italy, Tich celebrated by presenting the battalion with six puppies – all were adopted by soldiers.

One night near the Italian-Austrian frontier the battalion came under heavy fire and casualties mounted rapidly. For nine hours, with Tich at his side, Thomas carried out daring rescue work; together they brought back 30 badly wounded men, two or three at a time. 'We were bringing in the last two when a shell burst just ahead of us,' Thomas said. 'I went flying in one direction and Tich sailed off in another. When I came to I started yelling for Tich. Then I heard a muffled woof way off to my right. I dashed over and found Tich covered with rubble. I had to dig her out but, miraculously, she was not hurt badly.'

Rifleman Walker was awarded the Military Medal for his courage rescuing casualties under heavy fire, and Tich was recommended for the Dickin Medal by her Commanding Officer, who wrote: 'Her courage and devotion to duty were of very real and considerable value and her courageous example materially helped many men to keep their heads and sense of proportion in times of extreme danger. The sight of her put heart in the men as she habitually rode on the bonnet of her master's jeep and refused to leave her post even when bringing in wounded under heavy fire.' The Battalion's Chaplain said of Tich that: 'She can leap on to any type of truck or vehicle, will howl like a wolf, will cry, will remain standing against a wall until told to move. She will also smoke cigarettes, and never eat or drink until ordered to do so by her owner.'

After the war she lived with Thomas in Newcastle until her death in 1959. She was buried with full military honours in Ilford Pet Cemetery.

Her Dickin Medal is proudly displayed in the Royal Green Jackets (Rifles) Museum in Winchester.

Simon – Cat
HMS *Amethyst*
Date of Award: awarded posthumously 1949
Citation: *"Served on HMS Amethyst during the Yangtze Incident, disposing of many rats though wounded by shell blast. Throughout the incident his behaviour was of the highest order, although the blast was capable of making a hole over a foot in diameter in a steel plate."*

Simon's story is told in Chapter 7.

Chapter 3
JUDY'S STORY

Judy, a pedigree Pointer, was born at the Shanghai Dog Kennels, China, in 1936. She joined the Royal Navy and began her career as a ship's pet, aboard the Yangtze River Gunboat HMS *Gnat*. Practically her first act was to fall overboard into the Yangtze and nearly drown – not the most auspicious start for a dog destined to become a national heroine. At this time the Japanese had invaded China and were pushing up the Yangtze, and the gunboats had a difficult time trying to protect convoys. But this was a happy and relatively peaceful time for Judy, doted on by the crew and popular with everyone she met. At one point she was kidnapped by the crew of an American gunboat, who wanted her for their own, and only the most underhand actions by the *Gnat*'s crew (they stole the American boat's bell and held it to ransom) got her back. She met a handsome pointer dog, the ship's pet of a French gunboat, and following a solemn 'marriage' ceremony her first litter of puppies was born on the *Gnat*.

In 1939 she joined the crew of HMS *Grasshopper*, another gunboat, and at the end of that year the *Grasshopper* was sent to Singapore, where she saw active service in the Malaya-Singapore campaign. Judy's crewmates were impressed by her apparent ability to pick up incoming Japanese aircraft and 'point' to them before anyone else was aware of their approach. Despite Judy's best efforts, however, the war was not going well, and at the fall of Singapore in February 1942 HMS *Grasshopper*, laden with evacuees including women and children, headed for Java. Before it reached safety it was attacked by Japanese aircraft and badly damaged; desperately the crew beached the vessel as it broke up, leaving survivors floundering in the water or clinging to the wreckage of the ship. They struggled ashore to find themselves marooned on an uninhabited island with little food and no water. Judy had been trapped on the ship by falling debris, and was only rescued when the coxswain swam out the next day to the wreck to salvage what food and water he could. Once ashore Judy saved the day, and the crew, by sniffing out a fresh-water spring.

The resourceful group hitched a ride on a Chinese junk to the north-east coast of Sumatra. They decided to make for Padang, 200 miles away, where they hoped to join other British servicemen. They very nearly made it – but after a terrible five-week trek through thick jungle, with Judy constantly on guard, they arrived at Padang to find that they had missed the last departing ship by twenty-four hours. They were all, including Judy, taken prisoner.

Food rations were mean, and of course there was no ration for Judy; she and her shipmates became expert scroungers and Judy hunted for rats, snakes and birds. She had to be kept out of the way of the Japanese guards, and soon learned to disappear quietly when they were around. If they had but known it, Padang was a holiday camp compared to what was to come.

After a few months at Padang they were sent to the labour camp at Medan, on the north coast. The men were determined not to part with Judy and Petty Officer Puncheon covered her in rice sacks as they were herded onto the truck bound for Medan. For five days she remained quiet and undetected, slipping off the truck and disappearing into the jungle when the convoy halted.

Conditions at Medan were harsh and it may be that, in the daily struggle to survive, Judy's old crewmates had little time to spare for their loyal companion. At all events, it was at Medan that Judy met Leading Aircraftsman Frank Williams. He had seen her around the camp, scrounging for food, and in August 1942, he adopted her. He shared his daily handful of boiled rice with her and she never left his side. In fact, she deserted from the Navy and joined the Royal Air Force.

Many of the prisoners owed their lives to Judy. She kept an eye on everybody, warning the men if scorpions, poisonous snakes or crocodiles were around and even distracting the guards with displays of barking and aggression, helping some men escape a beating. She grew thinner, wilier, hunting to feed herself and sharing her unappetising catches with her fellow prisoners. And in the middle of this nightmare, Judy produced her second litter of puppies. No pampered pedigrees, this second litter, fathered by some unknown feral dog who had escaped the local cooking-pots; but the men loved them all the same, and even managed to pass them on in time to outside homes.

Judy hated the Japanese guards – and the feeling was mutual. Frank Williams had his work cut out talking the Japanese out of shooting her, and every time he confronted his captors he risked a beating himself. In an attempt to give her official protection, Frank hit on the notion of getting Judy registered as a Prisoner of War. Seizing his opportunity, he offered the Commandant one of the puppies as a present for a local lady of whom he was enamoured, and over a convivial drink Frank persuaded him to sign Judy's official papers. Later – sober, one presumes – he regretted his generosity, and hated both Frank and Judy with a passion thereafter; but his code of honour required him to stand by his word.

In June 1944, the Japanese decided to send their prisoners to Singapore. They were ordered aboard a merchant ship, the SS Van Warwyk; Judy was not supposed to go with them, but of course Frank had other ideas. He packed her into a rice sack and slung her upside down on his back. For three interminable, sweltering hours the men paraded in the tropical heat. Judy never moved and hardly breathed until finally the men were marched onto the ship and she was safely released into the ship's hold.

On the first day of the journey the ship was torpedoed and Frank, Judy and most of the other prisoners were trapped in a tangle of wreckage. Just as Judy struggled free, a second torpedo struck. Luckily, this explosion actually freed the trapped men, and they scrambled to abandon ship. Frank pushed Judy to safety through a 10-inch porthole before joining the scramble out of the hold. For the next two hours their lives hung in the balance as they drifted in the sea. Eventually they were all were picked up, but in the confusion Frank and Judy were separated. Witnesses told him they had seen her helping survivors by letting them cling to her as they struggled to reach pieces of wreckage. She was in the water for hours. It was an agonizing three days before the pair were reunited. In the meantime, Judy, in the care of a group of old friends from HMS *Grasshopper*, had an adventure of her own. Spotted on the docks in Singapore by a furious Japanese officer, she was ordered to be shot. Suddenly there was a shout – it was her old adversary, the Camp Commandant from Medan. Mindful of his agreement, he made it clear that Judy was to stay with the prisoners. Arriving at the prison camp, Judy refused to go into a hut with her old shipmates, and settled determinedly by the gate to wait for Frank. Frank later wrote '...as I entered the camp, a scraggy dog hit me square between the shoulders and knocked me over. Coated in bunker oil, her tired old eyes were bright red.' In July 1944, after four weeks in Singapore, they were sent back to Sumatra, where the Japanese were building a railway from Pekanbaru to Palembang, a distance of 138 miles. Conditions were every bit as appalling as on the Burma Railway; as many as ten men died a day, from starvation, malaria, infected tropical ulcers and a host of other conditions, and were buried along the route of the railway. Judy was a changed dog. She was no docile pet now; thin and hard, she faced a daily struggle for survival and learned to live on her wits and cunning. Without Frank, she may well have gone wild; without Judy, Frank may well have lain down and died, as did so many others. The bond between them was as strong as ever, and it kept them both going.

Judy was an inspiration to all the prisoners with her courage and determination. One wrote,

> *They would stagger to their work places*
> *Though they really ought to die*
> *And would mutter in their beards*
> *If that bitch can, so can I!*

Over the next few months, Frank and Judy moved from one camp to another, advancing through Sumatra with the railway. Rumours flew about that the war was nearly over, the Japanese nearly beaten. Their impending defeat seemed to make them more implacable, and they drove the prisoners mercilessly. Judy did her best; if a man was receiving a particularly severe beating she would bark furiously at the guard, snapping at his heels to distract him and then bolting for the jungle when he turned, raising his rifle.

The time had come for Judy to drop out of sight. She avoided detection by living her life between the camp and the relative safety of the jungle, while Frank communicated with her through a series of whistles. He still managed to smuggle a meagre ration of maggoty tapioca to her, and she supplemented this with snakes, rats and monkeys. She lived on the edge, still defying the Japanese guards to protect her friends and then melting back into the jungle. Always on the lookout for food, she must have been overwhelmed when she found an elephant's shinbone. It took her two hours to bury it. In this desperate fashion she survived until liberation came in 1945.

Ironically, even as a free dog, Judy's problems were not over. She was not invited aboard the troop-ship back to Liverpool, and Frank had to resort to smuggling her aboard again. With the men's help, Frank and Judy bamboozled the dock police and she was delivered to the ship's cook – who ensured she had more than her fair share of food in the galley.

Back in Britain, Judy had to endure six months in quarantine. She emerged a national heroine. News that she was to receive the Dickin Medal, and that she had been enrolled as the only dog member of the Returned British Prisoners of War Association in London, made her headline news around the world. In May 1946, Major Viscount Tarbat MC, chairman of the Returned British POW Association, fastened the bronze Dickin Medal to Judy's collar at a special ceremony.

Judy's citation reads: "For magnificent courage and endurance in Japanese prison camps, thus helping to maintain morale among her fellow prisoners and for saving many lives by her intelligence and watchfulness." At the same time Frank was awarded the PDSA's White Cross of St. Giles, the highest honour available, for his devotion to Judy.

But Judy's adventures didn't end there. Following demob, Frank was offered a position in East Africa on the Government's Groundnut Scheme. Naturally, dogs were not allowed on the flight, but following a plea from the Returned British POW Association and the PDSA, on the grounds of exceptional circumstances, permission was granted, and on 10th May 1948 Judy flew to Africa and a new life with Frank.

These were happy years for Judy; she loved her life in East Africa, loved being with Frank, and her third litter was born to peace and plenty.

But in February 1950 Judy went missing. Frank searched for days, and at last found her lying weak and helpless in a native hut. A tumour was diagnosed; an operation to remove it was successful, but infection set in and Judy had to be put to sleep.

Judy's grave in Tanganyika (now Tanzania) is marked by a granite memorial bearing a bronze plaque detailing her brave exploits in the war. It was Frank's final gesture of love and respect for the dog who proved over and over again that she was indeed man's best friend.

In 2006 relatives of Frank gave Judy's Dickin Medal, and her collar, to the Imperial War Museum in London. His widow said, 'It was Frank's wish for Judy's medal and collar to return to the PDSA before being presented to the Imperial War Museum, where her courage and devotion to duty will be remembered.'

They Also Serve

Chapter 4
THE HOME FRONT

While the armed services – and the dogs, horses, mules, camels and all the other creatures who accompanied them to war – fought across Europe, Africa and the Far East, on the home front the population, two-legged and four-legged, faced up to their own problems. Things were bad enough when the enemy was the constant shortage of food and other necessities; then the bombs came.

The Blitz was the darkest period in London's history, as German bombers sought to bring Britain to its knees by subjecting the capital to night after night of relentless bombing. Other cities, too, suffered horrifying raids: Coventry, Clydebank, Liverpool, Hull... almost no city in Britain escaped. And as the Civil Defence teams scrabbled desperately through the rubble hunting for survivors, dogs began to work alongside them.

Dogs have no doubt searched for and found their own lost masters since the beginning of the relationship between humans and canines, and the instinct is powerful enough for even an untrained dog to find and rescue people, as Sheila's story (told in Chapter 5) illustrates. The idea of training them specifically for the purpose, however, is of surprisingly recent date.

The famous St Bernards who worked at the Monastery at the summit of the St Bernard Pass were initially kept as guard dogs, then as guides accompanying the monks on their errands of mercy; but although they were credited with finding many lost travellers, locating missing persons was never their primary role.

During the First World War both sides used 'ambulance dogs' or 'mercy dogs', who carried first-aid kits strapped to their bodies, either acting as a pack-animal for a medical orderly or sent out on their own. Under the name 'Red Cross dogs' they were trained to find wounded soldiers. The French and the German armies were particularly keen in their use of dogs in this role.

As the Second World War began the work of these brave animals had faded from people's memories, but in the London Blitz the search-and-rescue dogs, while not yet called by that name, came into their own. The sustained bombing of London and other major cities from September 1940 caused widespread damage: as many as a million London homes were demolished or badly damaged, with the attendant horror of people, alive and dead, buried in the rubble. The job of finding them fell to the ARP (Air Raid Precautions) wardens, who were mostly older men considered unfit for military service, and, occasionally, to the dogs that accompanied them. At first many were simply eager, intelligent, untrained dogs – for example, Beauty and Rip, whose stories are told below – working alongside their masters and deciding to lend a hand; but their successes were so conspicuous that clearly such important work could not be left to strays and volunteers, and formal training soon got under way. The Civil Defence authorities began training dogs in urban search-and-rescue using techniques still practiced today. It is hard now to imagine a disaster, natural or man-made, earthquake or terrorist attack, where search-and-rescue dogs are not rushed immediately to the scene.

Search and rescue dogs can be classified according to whether or not they *scent discriminate*. Scent discriminating dogs alert only on the scent of an individual person, after being given a sample of that person's scent. Non-scent discriminating dogs alert on or follow any human scent, which is obviously what is required of a dog combing a disaster scene for survivors.

Also serving on the home front were the police horses of the Metropolitan Police, and three of them received the Dickin Medal for their steady devotion to duty. Going about their duties despite fires and explosions all around them, they became a much-loved symbol of the Londoner's stoical determination that life would go on as normally as possible under almost intolerable conditions.

The PDSA's Animal Rescue Squads swung into action, too, as the war began. The fleet of motor-caravan dispensaries were called in from their peace-time work and prepared, with their crews, to face the blitz. Caravans with specially trained volunteer personnel were based in the large cities where air raids were expected; the service was welcomed by the Civil Defence and the police, who of course could not be expected to devote time to rescuing animals when people were in need. With their proud slogan 'We Go Where The Bombs Fall' the Animal Rescue Squads rescued countless thousands of injured, terrified and homeless creatures; in London alone, at the height of the Blitz, more than 7,000 were saved in a single week. Creeping into cellars under bombed-out houses, climbing to upper floors hanging precariously over space, digging narrow tunnels through ruins and crawling through to the aid of some trapped or injured animal, the Rescue Squads left no call for help unanswered.

Many of the most successful search-and-rescue dogs were, and still are, German Shepherd dogs. As an entertaining little footnote to history, German Shepherd dogs were re-named 'Alsatians' during the war to save them from the possible stigma of being regarded as enemy aliens!

The stories of the Dickin Medal recipients who served on the home front follow.

Beauty – Wire-Haired Terrier
PDSA Rescue Squad
Date of Award: 12 January 1945
Citation: *"For being the pioneer dog in locating buried air-raid victims while serving with a PDSA Rescue Squad."*

During the Second World War the PDSA were kept busy caring for pets and other animals affected by the bombing. Bill Barnett was a member of the PDSA's animal rescue unit during the Blitz, on a squad dedicated to looking for animals trapped in the rubble after bomb blasts. His terrier Beauty was his constant companion, but he always thought of her as coming along just to provide him with company. Then one day in 1940 Beauty suddenly started to whine and scrabble in the rubble too; when the team went to investigate they uncovered a cat buried beneath a table.

From that day on Beauty was a working member of the team, going on to save 63 animals from being buried alive. Six other search-and-rescue dogs went on to receive the medal too, having followed Beauty's inspiring example. Beauty is often credited with being the first 'official' search-and-rescue dog.

Jet – Alsatian
MAP (Ministry of Aircraft Production) Serving with Civil Defence
Date of Award: 12 January 1945
Citation: *"For being responsible for the rescue of persons trapped under blitzed buildings while serving with the Civil Defence Services of London."*

Jet, donated by Mrs Hilda Cleaver, a patriotic owner in Liverpool, was trained as a guard dog at the War Dog School in Gloucester and was posted first to an airfield in Northern Ireland. Recalled to Gloucester, he underwent further training as a search dog; in training, some of the men were sent to hide and the dogs were then taken out and encouraged to find them. Jet succeeded magnificently, locating one man so well hidden he had been overlooked by the training squad and would have been left snug in his hidey-hole, and probably missed his tea when everyone else went home, if Jet hadn't refused orders to come back to base and stood stubbornly staring at the man's hiding-place. He worked next in Birmingham, on one occasion locating a woman who had been given up for dead by her family.

Soon he was sent to London to assist in search-and-rescue operations in the bombing, where he was teamed with Corporal Wardle, with whom he worked for the duration of the war. He was stationed at a barracks in Chelsea, where he often worked with Irma, another rescue dog who became a Dickin Medal winner. He took part in many searches, and became a well-known and welcome sight at the scene of any disaster, saving more than fifty people. Cpl Wardle said, 'Jet had an extraordinary keen scent and, as he stepped gingerly over the still-smoking ruins of a building, reduced to a heap of rubble by a Doodlebug, or V1 flying bomb, he would suddenly pause and sniff around one spot for a moment or two, until he was satisfied that he had a find, then he would indicate it by starting to dig. He was never known to give a wrong indication, but frequently burnt his feet by the attempted digging.'

On one memorable occasion in October 1944 he was sent to a hotel in Chelsea which had suffered a direct hit. The rescuers worked tirelessly, with Jet's constant assistance, until they thought everyone had been got out; the Civil Defence team were preparing to leave when Cpl Wardle called them back. 'There's someone still there,' he told them. 'High up.' The Civil Defence team were sceptical, but Cpl Wardle was insistent. 'If Jet says there's someone there, there's someone there,' he said firmly. 'And they're alive, by his behaviour.' Cpl Wardle had learned that if the person was dead Jet just sat, but if they were alive he continued to be agitated by whining and trying to get near them. Ladders were sent for, and the Civil Defence rescuers climbed up into the precarious building. They found a woman, alive, and thanks to Jet's determination, and his refusal to leave while there was still a soul to be saved, she was rescued. He had been at the scene nearly twelve hours. It was for this act of devotion to duty that Jet was nominated for the Dickin Medal. He is credited with saving around 50 people altogether.

After the war Jet retired and was living as a pet with Mrs Cleaver when in August 1947 there was a disastrous explosion in the William Colliery at Whitehaven in Cumbria. RAF Police dogs were enrolled to help in the search, and on their way north from Gloucester the party stopped to pick up Jet, considering him the most experienced dog available. The dogs (Jet, Prince and Rex) were taken underground to search for bodies. Sadly they found no survivors; but Jet saved the search party from serious injury or worse when he looked up, whined and moved back, refusing to go ahead and pulling them back just before a section of the roof collapsed.

Jet died in 1949 at 7 years of age.

Irma – Alsatian
MAP Serving with Civil Defence
Date of Award: 12 January 1945
Citation: *"For being responsible for the rescue of persons trapped under blitzed buildings while serving with the Civil Defences of London."*

Irma, who served with Jet, was credited with finding 191 people trapped under rubble during the bombing. Like Jet, Irma served not during the London Blitz of 1940-41 but in 1944-45 when London came under attack from V1 and V2 rockets.

On one occasion, in November 1944, she was called with her handler, Margaret Griffin, to the scene of a rocket attack at Shooter's Hill, South London, where a public house, an ambulance depot and several offices had been hit. Most of the casualties were in the bar and billiard room of the pub, but a few others were missing in the debris. Margaret put Irma in immediately, and she quickly identified an area of rubble. After two hours of digging, under 7 feet of rubble exactly where Irma had indicated, the bodies of two women were recovered.

On another occasion, in January 1945, they were working the scene of a rocket attack in West Ham when Irma suddenly began to indicate a site under the rubble, between the house and the road. Margaret called the rescue squad over and they began to dig. They found a woman and a little boy alive under the rubble – the search team had been walking all over that area and could have inadvertently crushed the victims if Irma had not found them in time.

Two weeks later they were called to the scene of another rocket attack, at Walthamstow, where four houses had been completely demolished and another dozen or so badly damaged. The search was hampered by burst water pipes and gas mains, but Irma again quickly indicated where to dig and after nearly two hours the team reached a woman with a baby and a little boy trapped in a Morrison shelter (a temporary shelter usually built under a solid table or in a safe corner). The woman, sadly, had died from suffocation; but the two children were brought out alive.

Margaret and her two dogs, Irma and Psyche, located a total of 233 people in bombed premises (Irma alone found 21 live victims and located 170 bodies). Irma had a trick of indicating whether victims she had located were alive or dead; she would bark and scrabble excitedly when she found a survivor, but would stand in silence simply indicating the location of the dead, and would lick at them when they were brought out from the rubble as if trying to bring them back to life.

Thorn – Alsatian
MAP Serving with Civil Defence
Date of Award: 2 March 1945
Citation: *"For locating air-raid casualties in spite of thick smoke in a burning building."*

Thorn was another Alsatian who worked bravely with the Civil Defence in search and rescue. Despite his heroism in dangerous conditions, however, he 'chickened out' when selected to take part in the Victory Parade in June 1946 and had to be withdrawn half-way through the parade!

Thorn came from a distinguished line of search and rescue dogs. He was spectacularly fearless and would dash into blazing buildings if he sensed anyone inside.

He once found a family trapped under a burning house. How he detected their scent baffled rescuers – but they got the family out alive.

Perhaps his courage under fire and his natural modesty are explained by the fact that he was said to be a direct descendent of Rin Tin Tin, the Hollywood star, who was rescued by an American serviceman as a puppy in France during the First World War.

Rex – Alsatian
MAP Civil Defence Rescue Dog
Date of Award: April 1945
Citation: *"For outstanding good work in the location of casualties in burning buildings. Undaunted by smouldering debris, thick smoke, intense heat and jets of water from fire hoses, this dog displayed uncanny intelligence and outstanding determination in his efforts to follow up any scent which led him to a trapped casualty."*

Rex, a handsome Alsatian, was another of the dogs who braved danger and discomfort to find casualties of the London bombing. In January 1945, while working in Lambeth, London, he homed in on an area already searched by rescue squads. He dug down, uncovering blood-soaked ground and then a buried bed. Rex pulled at the bedding and revealed casualties who would otherwise have been overlooked. He is recorded as having rescued more than 60 people from building debris. Such was his fame that when he died in 1954 at the age of 11 his passing was reported in newspapers throughout Britain. He is buried at the Ilford Cemetery.

Sheila – Collie
Date of Award: 2 July 1945
Citation: *"For assisting in the rescue of four American Airmen lost on the Cheviots in a blizzard after an air crash in December, 1944."*

Sheila's story is told in Chapter 5.

Rip – Mongrel
Stray picked up by Civil Defence Squad at Poplar, London E14
Date of Award: 1945
Citation: *"For locating many air-raid victims during the blitz of 1940."*

Rip, a scruffy little cross-breed, was one of the many strays made homeless by the bombing. These waifs were eager to find new owners, and many of them became mascots of fire stations, ambulance depots and Civil Defence units. Rip turned up one day as the local Civil Defence squad were at work around the London docks. One of the officers, Mr E. King, goodnaturedly offered the little dog a meal before shooing him away – or, at least, trying to. Rip wasn't going anywhere. If there was a job going as mascot of the Southill Street wardens, he was having it. He went with the squad on every mission; he quickly got the hang of what the men did and was soon sniffing and digging in the rubble and helping the team locate victims. He worked courageously through bombing raids, braving fire and smoke and collapsing buildings, and was completely unworried by the air-raid sirens. He would follow Mr King as he did his rounds; he soon became a familiar and popular sight in the streets around the docks, and people always had a quick pat and often a tasty titbit for him. He served for five years of the war, rescuing more than 100 people in 1940-41 alone, and in the autumn of 1946 this home front hero died peacefully in his sleep. He was buried in the PDSA pet cemetery at Ilford. His headstone says "Rip, D.M., 'We also serve' – for the dog whose body lies here played his part in the Battle of Britain."

Peter – Collie
Date of Award: November 1945
Citation: *"For locating victims trapped under blitzed buildings while serving with the MAP attached to Civil Defence of London."*

Peter, a Scottish collie, came with a bad reputation for fighting other dogs and destroying his owner's belongings. However, he found his niche in search and rescue work and became a reformed character. His service during the blitz was outstanding; he found six people buried alive in the ruins of their homes and the information he gave to his handler saved many lives. Peter was singled out for special attention at the Civil Defence Stand-Down parade in Hyde Park before the King and Queen and Princess Elizabeth in 1946. He was presented with his medal by Sir James Ross of the Air Ministry. He lived on to the age of 11 and is buried at Ilford cemetery.

Olga – Police Horse
Date of Award: 11 April 1947
Citation: *"On duty when a flying bomb demolished four houses in Tooting and a plate-glass window crashed immediately in front of her. Olga, after bolting for 100 yards, returned to the scene of the incident and remained on duty with her rider, controlling traffic and assisting rescue organisations."*

The Metropolitan Police horses were initially evacuated from London to the countryside, but were soon brought back onto the streets. It is worth bearing in mind that horses have a natural fear and loathing of so many of the things that the Metropolitan Police horses were subjected to during the Blitz – explosions, loud noises, fire. Their steadfast service is all the more remarkable in view of this.

Bay mare Olga had been on patrol in Tooting, South London, when a German flying bomb exploded, destroying a row of houses and sending debris flying. When a sheet of glass crashed at her feet, she bolted in panic, but controlled her fear to return to duty, helping officers to restore order and assisting in the search for people buried in the rubble.

Regal – Police Horse
Date of Award: 11 April 1947
Citation: *"Was twice in burning stables caused by explosive incendiaries at Muswell Hill. Although receiving minor injuries, being covered by debris and close to the flames, this horse showed no signs of panic."*

In the north London suburb of Muswell Hill, Regal faced experiences in common with so many blitzed Londoners. A cluster of incendiary bombs fell close to his stable but Regal remained calm and was led to safety. Three years later a second bomb landed so close that part of his stable was damaged. Again he behaved with great courage and composure.

Upstart – Police Horse
Date of Award: 11 April 1947
Citation: *"While on patrol duty in Bethnal Green a flying bomb exploded within 75 yards, showering both horse and rider with broken glass and debris. Upstart was completely unperturbed and remained quietly on duty with his rider controlling traffic, etc., until the incident had been dealt with."*

Upstart was on duty in Bethnal Green in the East End when a flying bomb exploded close by, bringing debris crashing down around horse and rider. He kept calm, probably because he was stabled at Hyde Park near anti-aircraft batteries, and had grown accustomed to loud noises. His sturdy assurance was of great help as his rider directed emergency services to the scene.

Olga, Regal and Upstart received the Dickin Medal on behalf of the 186 horses of the Metropolitan Police Mounted Branch.

They Also Serve

Chapter 5
SHEILA'S STORY

The Cheviot Hills lie on the border between Scotland and England, a stark and beautiful landscape of wide moors and heather-clad mountains. It was at Dunsdale in these hills that shepherd John Dagg lived and worked with his collie, Sheila. A veteran of the bitter fighting of the First World War, when he served in the King's Own Scottish Borderers, John was content to do his part in the Second by working on the land, out and about with Sheila in all weathers, tending the flocks.

The war was at its height, and Britain was temporarily home to many American servicemen, including the airmen of the 303rd Bomb Group. On the morning of 16th December 1944, thirty-nine B-17 Flying Fortresses of the 303rd BG took off from RAF Molesworth in Cambridgeshire in wintry weather on a bombing raid on the railway marshalling yards at Ulm. Over the North Sea, the weather proved too much for the operation and the flight was recalled at 10.05 am. The aircraft broke formation on the return route and were ordered to land separately at various airfields, partly to avoid the danger of mid-air collisions. Many of the aircraft jettisoned their bombs over the North Sea as they made their way back to base; the majority landed safely at an RAF airfield at Kirmington, in Lincolnshire.

They Also Serve

When the flight was recalled the pilot of B-17 No.44-6504, 2nd Lt George A. Kyle, turned back towards England and soon found himself separated from the rest of the flight. Several times he requested headings, only to discover that they were deliberately false signals coming from German transmitters. Twice he found himself heading toward France. Hopelessly lost, and not knowing whether he was over land or sea, he did not dare to jettison his bombs in case they fell on some English town or village below. By now, although he did not know it, he was much too far north to find any of the airfields the flight were making for.

Cautiously he descended to 3,000 ft., trying to find a gap in the clouds to get his bearings. At a quarter past one the shoulder of The Cheviot, at 2,650 ft. one of the highest mountains in England outside the Lake District, suddenly loomed out of the swirling snow. The B-17 had nowhere to go.

The plane struck the mountainside and skidded across a peat bog, the soft ground fortunately absorbing some of the impact. The fuselage was torn and twisted, and fires broke out as fuel and hydraulic fluid spilled from ruptured pipes. Two of the nine-man crew were killed in the crash. The pilot and co-pilot, along with the third member of the cockpit crew, managed to scramble out of the wreckage; disorientated, not knowing if they were the only survivors, they stumbled off into the deep snow and the blizzard. They soon lost sight of the plane. Eventually they managed to find their way down the mountain to a farmhouse and safety.

Four men were left in the fuselage of the aircraft, all suffering minor injuries. Sgt J.A. Berly tried desperately to fight the fire, but the damaged floor of the aircraft suddenly gave way and he fell through, trapping his leg. Sgt William Kaufmann was knocked out in the crash, but regained consciousness in time to pull Sgt Berly free, and with Sgt George Smith they crawled out of the plane. They found tail-gunner Sgt Howard Delany staggering in the deep snow, dazed and bleeding from a severe head wound. Knowing they had to get away from the aircraft because of the risk of an explosion, the four injured men fought their way through the howling wind until, unable to go any further, they took refuge in a ditch 100 yards away. Exhausted, they huddled together in their pitiful shelter.

Away down the mountain, John Dagg heard the crash and knew immediately that it was a plane down. Without hesitation he called Sheila to him, and set off through the appalling conditions to look for survivors and see what he could do to help. Drawing on his knowledge of the area he headed in the direction of Braydon Crags high on The Cheviot. On his way, as he toiled up the hill in the driving snow with Sheila at his side, he met young shepherd Frank Moscrop, of Southernknowe. Frank too had heard the crash, and the two men, with the collie beside them, trudged up the mountain in the teeth of the snowstorm. In the whiteout conditions, and with the daylight already beginning to fade, finding even something the size of a Flying Fortress was going to be a formidable task. It could be a long search; and there was a real risk that any survivors would have perished before help arrived. While her master and Frank Moscrop hunted for the crash site in the blinding snow and gathering darkness, Sheila disappeared into the storm.

After several hours huddled in the ditch, George Smith, drifting between sleep and unconsciousness, was startled to suddenly feel something warm and wet on his cheek. A dog was licking his face! As the aircrew exclaimed in wonder Sheila set up a determined barking, which soon brought the two shepherds hurrying to the scene. Crouching in the ditch, John administered what first-aid he could to the wounded airmen. When they had got them patched up as well as they could, John and Frank held a quick conference. They decided that it would be better to try and get the airmen off the mountain as quickly as possible, rather than leaving them and going to bring help. Wrapping the injured men's feet carefully in parachute silk, the shepherds set off into the whiteout, assisting the Americans as much as they could. It was going to be a difficult journey; as the conditions worsened, even the two shepherds, who knew the mountain well, could easily get lost. Trusting to Sheila's sense of direction they followed her through the blizzard and the snowdrifts. Without her they could have wandered for hours, but she led them confidently on through the swirling snow. In the appalling conditions, and with four wounded men to help, it was a painfully slow journey, but at last they made it back to John's remote homestead. Just as they reached there the bombs still aboard the B-17 away behind them up on the hill exploded, with enough force to rattle the windows of the cottage.

As the airmen rested thankfully by the cottage fireside John's young daughter ran two miles through the storm to summon help by telephone. Later that night the four sergeants were taken to the same RAF hospital that had treated the cockpit crew earlier in the day.

For the heroic rescue, both man and dog received bravery awards at a unique joint ceremony. John Dagg, along with Frank Moscrop, got the British Empire Medal for Meritorious Service and Sheila was given the Dickin Medal for Gallantry, accepting it, according to observers, 'somewhat unwillingly'. According to a citation in the London Gazette: 'There is little doubt that their bravery, skill and determination were instrumental in saving the lives of four airmen by exposure.' Unusually, Sheila was recommended for the Dickin Medal by the Home Office and received the award, signed by Maria Dickin, at a hillside ceremony in July 1945. Her master received his BEM at the same time – the only instance of simultaneous gallantry awards to man and dog. Sheila was also the first 'civilian' dog to receive the Dickin Medal.

In 1946, the mother of one of the two men who had died in the crash wrote to John and thanked him for his efforts on behalf of the crew. She asked that if Sheila had puppies, she would like to buy one. A few months later the RAF flew Sheila's first puppy, named Tibbie, to South Carolina. Tibbie lived for 11 years as the adopted town pet of Columbia, SC.

The wreckage of the bomber still lies strewn on the mountain, a mute reminder of a time when war came even to the remote mountains of the Border.

A monument to all airmen who lost their lives on the Cheviot Hills was erected on 19th May 1995. The dedication ceremony was attended by crash survivors George Kyle and Joe Berly, and by Frank Moscrop.

George Kyle died in 2005 and, at his request, his ashes were scattered at the site of the crash in the bleak northern hills of England, where four of his friends and crewmates would have lost their lives but for the courage and determination of a sheepdog called Sheila.

Chapter 6
THE FLYING SQUAD

Messenger pigeons were extensively used in the First World War; 100,000 of them served, with an incredible rate of success. Barring the hazards of war, over 95% of them got their messages through. The pigeon's homing ability has always made it useful as a messenger, and the discovery that pigeons can be trained to 'follow' a mobile loft, homing to the loft itself rather than to a geographical location, increased their military value tenfold. In 1914, during the battle of the Marne, the French army had 72 mobile pigeon lofts which advanced with them. Even pigeons which were out on a mission when their loft was moved found their way back to it.

The US also used pigeons in France. One American pigeon, Cher Ami, was awarded the French Croix de Guerre with Palm for heroism during the Battle of Verdun. On his final mission he flew 25 miles in as many minutes to deliver his message (his twelfth during the battle) despite serious injuries – shot through the breast and wing, and with one leg shot off. The crucial message was retrieved from the canister hanging from the ligament of his severed leg, and saved 194 soldiers of the 'Lost Battalion' of the 77th Infantry Division.

At the outbreak of the Second World War the National Pigeon Service was formed to organise the involvement of racing pigeons into the war effort. Thousands of Britain's pigeon fanciers donated their birds; during the war nearly a quarter of a million pigeons were used as message carriers by the army, the RAF and the Civil Defence Services, including the police, the fire service and the Home Guard. Pigeon racing was suspended for the duration, and all along the coasts of Britain birds of prey were culled so that serving messenger pigeons could arrive home safely. Pigeons carried their messages either in containers on their legs or small pouches looped over their backs. Pigeons were dropped by parachute in containers to Resistance workers in France, Belgium and Holland. All RAF bombers and reconnaissance aircraft carried pigeons, in special watertight baskets and containers; if the aircraft had to ditch in the sea its location could be sent back by pigeon to its RAF base and a search and rescue operation mounted. Hundreds of airmen's lives were saved by these gallant birds, who often flew in the most extreme conditions. The first two Dickin Medal winners, Winkie and White Vision, came from this branch of the service.

From the outbreak of the War, pigeons played a vital role in the war effort, providing an invaluable message service which both saved lives and contributed to the effectiveness of military operations. They were used not only by British forces in Western Europe but also by American, Canadian, and German forces and in other parts of the world. Pigeons saw service in Italy, Greece, North Africa, India and the Middle and Far East. During 1939-45 over 200,000 young pigeons were given to the services by the British pigeon breeders of the NPS.

The birds were used by the RAF and the Army and Intelligence Services, Special Section of the Army Pigeon Service. During three and a half years of the Second World War, 16,554 'war pigeons' were parachuted onto the continent.

In 2012 Mr David Martin was doing some home improvements in his Surrey home when he came upon the skeleton of a veteran carrier pigeon – in his chimney. The bird still had a secret coded message from the Second World War in a red capsule attached to its leg. The code has so far defied all attempts to crack it. Bletchley Park (or at least their permanent 'Pigeons at War' exhibition) are on the case.

Of the 53 Dickin Medals awarded for service in the Second World War, 32 went to pigeons. Their stories are a humbling reminder of how much our soldiers, airmen and seamen owed to these brave, uncomplaining messengers.

Winkie

Pigeon NEHU.40.NS.1
Date of Award: 2 December 1943
Citation: *"For delivering a message under exceptionally difficult conditions and so contributing to the rescue of an Air Crew while serving with the RAF in February, 1942."*

The first pigeon to win the Dickin Medal was Winkie, a blue chequered hen. She was a messenger pigeon based at RAF Leuchars on the east coast of Scotland. On 23rd February 1942, she was aboard a Beaufort bomber making a strike against enemy positions in Norway. The plane had been critically damaged in the raid and as they turned for home, the crew were struggling to keep the aircraft in the air. As it limped home over the North Sea through a bitterly cold winter night, the plane shook and rattled helplessly; suddenly the water was rushing up to meet them and the plane crashed and broke up in the freezing waters of the North Sea. As the crew scrambled for the life-raft Winkie broke free from her cage.

Back at Leuchars, it was known that the plane had ditched, but they had no bearings for the crash; nevertheless a search was mounted, without much hope of success.

Struggling out of the icy, oil-slicked sea, her wings clogged with oily water, Winkie nevertheless flew back to her loft 129 miles away. Shortly before dawn, Winkie arrived, wet and bedraggled, in her loft in Broughty Ferry, near Dundee. Her owner, George Ross, immediately informed RAF Leuchars.

Though she carried no message (having escaped from her cage, rather than being released with a message), Sgt Davidson of the RAF pigeon service was able to work out how long she had been flying for and how many miles she may have covered; and this, combined with the last known position of the aircraft, the wind speed and the state of her oily feathers (which would have affected her speed), enabled him to direct the search to the right area. A rescue team was sent out to the downed plane and the crew, huddled shivering in a dinghy, were saved.

It was the first such rescue, by pigeon, in the War – but not the last.

In 1943 the rescued crew of the Beaufort bomber held a dinner for Winkie, who basked in her cage among the silver and crystal on the dining-table as she was toasted by the officers.

Winkie was returned to her owner after the war, and when she died he donated her (suitably stuffed) and her Dickin Medal to Dundee Art Galleries and Museums.

White Vision
Pigeon SURP.41.L.3089
Date of Award: 2 December 1943
Citation: *"For delivering a message under exceptionally difficult conditions and so contributing to the rescue of an Air Crew while serving with the RAF in October 1943."*

One morning in October 1943 a Catalina flying boat of 190 Squadron Royal Air Force, piloted by Flying Officer Ron Vaughan, set out from Sullom Voe in the Shetland Islands with a crew of eleven – and two pigeons aboard. They were patrolling the northern seas looking for U-Boats. Towards the end of the flight the plane was diverted to Aberdeen, as the airfield at Sullom Voe was closed down by bad weather; but conditions were just as bad at Aberdeen and they were diverted again, this time to Oban, on the west coast.

With fuel running low, however, after 21 hours in the air things were desperate; and before the Catalina could reach Oban she ran out of fuel and ditched in the sea off the Hebrides. Unable to make radio contact, Flying Officer Vaughan put details of their location into the leg capsule of each pigeon and sent them off, before turning his attention to evacuating the wallowing aircraft. A further disaster now struck, when one of the two life-rafts was carried off by the sea with only two men aboard. The single raft left would not hold the remaining nine men, and they elected to stay in the plane – a flying boat, of course, stood a greater chance of staying afloat than would a normal aircraft.

One of the pigeons failed to make it home, but White Vision battled on for 60 miles against the gale force wind, with visibility rarely above 100 yards, and at about 5 o'clock that afternoon she arrived exhausted at her loft. With the information she brought, the search was now on and the entire crew was rescued, about forty hours after they had ditched. As the last man jumped the gap between the stricken plane and the launch, the plane sank. The two men who had drifted off in the life-raft were picked up later, so White Vision saved her entire crew.

Aircrew often joked about their pigeons, and the possibility of dining off roast pigeon if their flying rations were cut. One imagines the men of that particular Catalina were thankful they hadn't snacked on their brave little bird.

White Vision survived the war and lived on until 1953.

The Walt Disney animated film *Valiant* was inspired by the life and times of Winkie and White Vision and their fellows in the National Pigeon Service.

Tyke (also known as George)
Pigeon Number 1263 MEPS 43
Date of Award: 2 December 1943
Citation: *"For delivering a message under exceptionally difficult conditions and so contributing to the rescue of an Air Crew, while serving with the RAF in the Mediterranean in June, 1943."*

Tyke was reared in Cairo and served with the Middle East Pigeon Service. Unlike Winkie and White Vision he did not have to face the ferocity of the North Sea, but the war in the desert presented its own problems: extreme heat by day and cold by night, and the constant misery of sandstorms. In June 1943, Tyke carried a message in poor visibility around 100 miles to his base, as a result of which an aircrew was rescued. Afterwards the men claimed they owed their lives to the pigeon.

Beach Comber
Pigeon NPS.41.NS.4230
Date of Award: 6 March 1944
Citation: *"For bringing the first news to this country of the landing at Dieppe, under hazardous conditions in September, 1942, while serving with the Canadian Army."*

On 19th August 1942 over 6,000 Allied troops, predominantly Canadian, supported by large naval and air force contingents, attacked the German-occupied port of Dieppe on the northern coast of France. The raid, dogged by confused planning, bad weather and inadequate air support, was doomed from the outset.

The objective was to seize and hold a major port for a short period, to assess the German strength and to gather intelligence from prisoners and captured materials. The raid was not a success. The troops came under heavy fire and within a few hours over 3,500 were killed, wounded, or captured.

For reasons of secrecy, it was inadvisable to use wireless, and two pigeons were set free on Dieppe beach, each with the first news of the operations. One pigeon was almost immediately shot down, but the other, Beach Comber, flew out through a barrage of fire, bringing the first news of the battle at an average speed of 50 miles an hour and enabling swift tactical decisions to be made and the raid to be called off.

Within ten hours of the first landings it was all over. Casualty rates were appalling, with over 60% of those who landed either killed, wounded or captured. Without Beach Comber's message, things could have been even worse.

Gustav

Pigeon NPS.42.31066
Date of Award: 1 September 1944
Citation: *"For delivering the first message from the Normandy Beaches from a ship off the beach-head while serving with the RAF on 6 June 1944."*

Gustav, trained by Frederick Jackson, of Cosham, Portsmouth, was the first pigeon to bring back news of D-Day to the UK. He was one of six carrier pigeons assigned by the RAF to Reuters war correspondent Montague Taylor, who crossed the English Channel with Allied Forces. The birds were carried into battle in wicker baskets on servicemen's backs and set free to fly home with vital information.

Gustav was released from a ship off the Normandy beaches and flew 150 miles to his loft at Thorney Island, near Portsmouth, against headwinds of up to 30mph. The day was overcast, and there was no sun to guide him. The journey lasted five hours and 16 minutes.

His handler, Sgt Harry Halsey took the message that read: 'We are just 20 miles or so off the beaches. First assault troops landed 0750. Signal says no interference from enemy gunfire on beach... Steaming steadily in formation. Lightnings, Typhoons, Fortresses crossing since 0545. No enemy aircraft seen.'

Ironically, Gustav survived the war only to killed when his owner trod on him while cleaning out the loft. Sometimes danger lurks in the most unexpected places.

Paddy

Pigeon NPS.43.9451
Date of Award: 1 September 1944
Citation: *"For the best recorded time with a message from the Normandy Operations, while serving with the RAF in June, 1944."*

Messenger pigeon Paddy, who was bred in Larne, Northern Ireland, made the fastest recorded crossing of the English Channel, carrying vital messages from Normandy following the D-Day landings. Paddy was based at RAF Hurn in Hampshire, and was among 30 pigeons taken to France by a unit of the 1st US Army during the Normandy landings on 6th June 1944. Paddy was released at 8.15 am on 12th June, carrying coded information on the Allied advance, and travelled 230 miles back to RAF Hurn in 4 hours 50 minutes. Paddy, who lived to the age of 11, is to date the only Irish recipient of the Dickin Medal.

Kenley Lass
Pigeon NURP.36.JH.190
Date of Award: March 1945
Citation: *"For being the first pigeon to be used with success for secret communications from an Agent in enemy-occupied France while serving with the NPS in October 1940."*

Kenley Lass was sent with a secret agent known as "Phillipe" into France in October 1940. Dropped by parachute, Phillipe's brief was to contact the resistance movement and gather as much information as possible for action against the occupying Germans. Radio could not be used as it would have given away his position to the Germans, so he carried two pigeons in his backpack, carefully packed in old socks with the toes cut off and the birds' heads sticking out of the holes. This was apparently considered sufficient to protect them during the landing! Phillipe was a Frenchman, and was familiar with the area; he had a friend in the vicinity who had a now-empty pigeon loft (the German occupiers had forbidden the keeping of pigeons, knowing they could be used for communications) where the two birds could be kept safe from prying eyes.

Despite having no previous experience with pigeons Phillipe had been well instructed, and after 10 days he sent Kenley Lass off with her message at 8.20 in the morning of 20th October 1940. She arrived home at her loft in East Grinstead at 3.00 in the afternoon, having flown 300 miles to carry her important information.

On 16th February 1941 she was sent to France again on a repeat mission, returning home in excellent time again four days later with further information.

Dutch Coast
Pigeon NURP.41. A.2164
Date of Award: March 1945
Citation: *"For delivering an SOS from a ditched Air Crew close to the enemy coast 288 miles distance in 7½ hours, under unfavourable conditions, while serving with the RAF in April 1942."*

Like Winkie and White Vision, Dutch Coast was one of the pigeons who took part in RAF operations, carried on bombers as a last line of communication if radios were inoperable. He battled back to his loft through appalling weather to bring word of the location of the crew of an aircraft which had crashed into the sea, enabling a search and rescue operation to be launched and his crew saved.

Navy Blue
Pigeon NPS.41.NS.2862
Date of Award: March 1945
Citation: *"For delivering an important message from a Raiding Party on the West Coast of France, although injured, while serving with the RAF in June, 1944."*

Navy Blue worked with the RAF on air-sea rescue service, where he had assisted with many rescues. Because of his excellent record, he was selected for a special mission: he was to take part in a seaborne landing by a small reconnaissance party on the west coast of France. The mission departed on 15th June 1944, just nine days after D-Day, with Navy Blue in a small container, but the landing did not take place until the night of 17th-18th June. Navy Blue spent more than two days confined in his tiny container, unable to stretch his wings. Sent off with a vital message to the Intelligence Branch, he flew some 200 miles to his base at Plymouth, arriving injured and exhausted at 2.45 in the morning on 19th June (the message did not give the time of his release, so it is not known how long the flight took him). Despite his wounds, he got his message through in the critical days after the D-Day landings.

Ruhr Express
Pigeon NPS.43.29018
Date of Award: May 1945
Citation: *"For carrying an important message from the Ruhr Pocket in excellent time, while serving with the RAF in April, 1945."*

In April 1945 the German army was on the retreat and pressure was on them to surrender. At this stage of the war Ruhr Express was dropped behind German lines and was promptly captured. Narrowly avoiding being cooked and eaten by hungry soldiers, the pigeon was delivered to the local German command Headquarters. The Germans were by this time well aware that the end was in sight, and the commandant made the decision to release the pigeon with 'very valuable information... considered to have had a direct influence on the progress of the war at that crucial time.' Ruhr Express carried this vital information some 300 miles (480 km) to his London loft. The flight across the North Sea had been made in record time.

In September 1945 he was auctioned, along with his Dickin Medal, in aid of the RAF Benevolent Fund. He raised the astonishing sum of £420. In 1994 Ruhr Express was sold again (stuffed, this time), and he and his medal made £5,800.

Flying Dutchman
Pigeon – NPS.42.NS.44802
Date of Award: March 1945
Citation: *"For successfully delivering messages from Agents in Holland on three occasions. Missing on fourth mission, while serving with the RAF in 1944."*

Flying Dutchman, a dark chequered cock, was lost in action over the North Sea on his way back from Holland to his loft in Felixstowe. Like so many of his fellows Flying Dutchman gave everything in the performance of the duties for which he had been trained, and in support of the war effort.

Commando
Pigeon NURP.38.EGU.242
Date of Award: March 1945
Citation: *"For successfully delivering messages from Agents in Occupied France on three occasions: twice under exceptionally adverse conditions, while serving with the NPS in 1942."*

Sid Moon had served with the Army Pigeon Service during the First World War, and on the outbreak of war in 1939 he immediately made his pigeons available again. Commando, a red chequered pigeon, was one of the birds he had bred before the war at his loft in Haywards Heath, West Sussex, and trained as a homing pigeon.

In the dark days of 1942, Britain was suffering German bombing and was under constant threat of invasion. Contact with Special Operations Executive agents across Europe was fraught with difficulties; radios were not always reliable, and the Germans ruthlessly hunted down wireless operators. Pigeons, too, were in constant danger from marksmen and falconers stationed along the Channel coast to bring them down. Between enemy action, bad weather and exhaustion, probably fewer than one in eight was successful in making it home.

Parachuted into France by the secret Special Operations Executive, Commando flew crucial intelligence, strapped to his leg in a tiny canister, back to Britain on no less than three missions, in June, August and September of 1942. The information revealed the location of German troops, industrial sites and injured British soldiers. For his "conspicuous bravery and devotion" he was presented with his Dickin Medal, along with fellow pigeon Royal Blue, by Rear Admiral R.M. Bellairs in 1945.

Commando's medal sold in 2004 for £9,200.

Royal Blue
Pigeon NURP.40.GVIS.453
Date of award: March 1945
Citation: *"For being the first pigeon in this war to deliver a message from a forced landed aircraft on the Continent while serving with the RAF in October, 1940."*

King George VI kept up family tradition by maintaining pigeon lofts at Sandringham, the Royal Family's country home in Norfolk, and at the outbreak of the Second World War he volunteered his birds for service with the NPS. Bred in the Royal Loft at Sandringham, Royal Blue was serving on an aircraft which force-landed in Holland on 10th October 1940. Released at 7.20 in the morning, Royal Blue was home in his loft at 11.30, having covered 120 miles in 4 hours 10 minutes, bringing information about the situation of the crew. It was the first time a pigeon had delivered information about a forced-landed crew.

William of Orange
Pigeon NPS.42.NS.15125
Date of Award: May 1945
Citation: *"For delivering a message from the Arnhem Airborne Operation in record time for any single pigeon, while serving with the APS in September 1944."*

William of Orange was bred in Cheshire by Sir William Proctor Smith, and saw service at the Battle of Arnhem. In this battle, troops were airlifted, by glider and parachute, behind enemy lines.

The Battle of Arnhem is renowned for its communications failures. The airborne forces, surrounded by German troops and desperate to get information out of the battle zone, found that the few radio sets they had with them malfunctioned. William of Orange was released from Arnhem, with a message fixed to his leg, at 10.30 in the morning on 19th September 1944 and arrived at his loft in England at 2.55 that afternoon, having flown over 250 miles – 135 of them over open sea – in 4 hours 25 minutes. It was one of the few messages to make its way back from Arnhem to the UK.

Sir William bought him back from the Army after the war, and his progeny went on to become fine racing pigeons; but few of them will have equalled their famous ancestor's epic flight. Lady Smith presented William of Orange's Dickin Medal to the Royal Signals Museum in 1965.

Scotch Lass
Pigeon NPS.42.21610
Date of Award: June 1945
Citation: *"For bringing 38 microphotographs across the North Sea in good time although injured, while serving with the RAF in Holland in September 1944."*

An experienced pigeon with 43 missions under her belt (or tied around her leg, anyway), Scotch Lass was dropped with a secret agent in the Netherlands on the early morning of 12th September 1944. She was released with valuable information contained in 38 microphotographs taken by Dutch resistance workers. Despite being wounded as she flew into telegraph wires in the half-light, she got going again and reached England to deliver her information.

The use of the new technology of microphotography meant that far more information could be carried than could have previously been carried by one pigeon.

Billy
Pigeon NU.41.HQ.4373
Date of Award: August 1945
Citation: *"For delivering a message from a force-landed bomber, while in a state of complete collapse and under exceptionally bad weather conditions, while serving with the RAF in 1942."*

Broad Arrow
Pigeon 41.BA.2793
Date of Award: October 1945
Citation: *"For bringing important messages three times from enemy occupied country, viz: May 1943, June 1943 and August 1943, while serving with the Special Service from the Continent."*

Pigeon NPS.42.NS.2780
Date of Award: October 1945
Citation: *"For bringing important messages three times from enemy occupied country, viz: July 1942, August 1942 and April 1943, while serving with the Special Service from the Continent."*

Pigeon NPS.42.NS.7524
Date of Award: October 1945
Citation: *"For bringing important messages three times from enemy-occupied country, viz: July 1942, May 1943 and July 1943, while serving with the Special Service from the continent."*

Maquis
Pigeon NPSNS.42.36392
Date of Award: October 1945
Citation: *"For bringing important messages three times from enemy occupied country, viz: May 1943 (Amiens) February, 1944 (Combined Operations) and June, 1944 (French Maquis) while serving with the Special Service from the Continent."*

Maquis, a blue chequered cock, was dropped behind enemy lines three times to bring information back to Britain. His missions, vital to the war effort, were flown in difficult and often dangerous conditions.

Mary
Pigeon NURP.40.WCE.249
Date of Award: November 1945
Citation: *"For outstanding endurance on War Service in spite of wounds."*

One of the most famous English military pigeons was Mary of Exeter, a racing pigeon belonging to Charlie Brewer, a shoemaker in Exeter, Devon. Many of Charlie's pigeons served in the War, often relaying highly secret information, and he was sworn to the strictest secrecy.

Mary joined the National Pigeon Service in 1940 and flew repeated missions during the next five years. She was dropped into France on four occasions, each time making her way home with her message despite injuries. On her first mission she was shot. On another, in 1942, she was attacked by a hawk and part of her wing was ripped off; she needed seven stitches when she got home. Each time she was nursed back to health and returned to action. A few months later she was shot again, and on her return three shotgun pellets were removed surgically and she was stitched up again.

Recuperating at home from her third injury in the line of duty, she was caught in a bombing raid during the Exeter blitz and her loft was blown to bits. She was missing for ten days, and was picked up in a nearby field, nearly dead with severe shrapnel wounds to her head and neck. Her neck muscles were so badly damaged the resourceful Charlie used his shoemaking skills to fashion her a little leather collar to support her neck. In total this brave little bird was wounded four times and received 22 stitches

Mary was awarded her Dickin Medal in 1945 and lived on until 1950. She is buried, with her collar, in Ilford Cemetery.

Tommy
Pigeon NURP.41.DHZ56
Date of Award: February 1946
Citation: *"For delivering a valuable message from Holland to Lancashire under difficult conditions, while serving with NPS in July 1942."*

Tommy, a racing pigeon from Dalton-in-Furness in Lancashire, managed to get lost over the continent in 1942, and fell fortuitously into the hands of the Dutch resistance. When they discovered vital information about a German U-Boat base they sent Tommy off to carry the information to Britain. He came under heavy and sustained fire from German soldiers, but won through and brought his message home.

His owner, puzzled by the message attached to his leg, handed it to the police, who recognized its importance and made sure it was delivered to the proper authorities. As a result the RAF were able to carry out a successful bombing raid on the U-boat base.

All Alone
Pigeon NURP.39.SDS.39
Date of Award: February 1946
Citation: *"For delivering an important message in one day over a distance of 400 miles, while serving with the NPS in August, 1943."*

In the summer of 1943, All Alone, a blue hen, parachuted into France with a British agent. The agent learned important information about the Milice, a Vichy paramilitary group whose mission was to round up Jews for deportation and to attack the French Resistance.

All Alone carried this information more than four hundred miles, across the English Channel, back to her home in Staines, Middlesex, in less than twenty-four hours. The speed of her flight and the importance of its information of its success earned All Alone her Dickin Medal.

Princess
Pigeon 42WD593
Date of Award: May 1946
Citation: *"Sent on special mission to Crete, this pigeon returned to her loft (RAF Alexandria) having travelled about 500 miles mostly over sea, with most valuable information. One of the finest performances in the war record of the Pigeon Service."*

Mercury
Pigeon NURP.37.CEN.335
Date of Award: August 1946
Citation: *"For carrying out a special task involving a flight of 480 miles from Northern Denmark while serving with the Special Section Army Pigeon Service in July 1942."*

Pigeon NURP.38.BPC.6.
Date of Award: August 1946
Citation: *"For three outstanding flights from France while serving with the Special Section, Army Pigeon Service, 11 July 1941, 9 September 1941, and 29 November 1941."*

GI Joe
Pigeon USA43SC6390
Date of Award: August 1946
Citation: *"This bird is credited with making the most outstanding flight by a USA Army Pigeon in World War II. Making the 20 mile flight from British 10th Army HQ, in the same number of minutes, it brought a message which arrived just in time to save the lives of at least 100 Allied soldiers from being bombed by their own planes."*

A blue chequer bird, G.I. Joe was raised and trained by American forces in North Africa. In 1943 he was on duty with British Tenth Corps in Italy. The 56th Infantry was preparing to take the German-held town of Colvi Vecchia, and had requested air support from the Americans to bombard German positions before they made their advance on the town. On 18th October 1943 the Germans unexpectedly retreated, leaving only a small rearguard, and the British troops broke through and captured the town ahead of the scheduled attack. Of course, the priority now was to stop the American bombing raid; but radio communication could not be established. If the American attack came now, the British troops in the town would be bombed. G.I. Joe was dispatched on a do-or-die mission. He flew twenty miles in 22 minutes, arriving as the engines of the bombers were warming up. Had he arrived just five minutes later many of the British troops in the town would have been killed or injured.

In 1946 G.I. Joe came to Britain to receive his Dickin Medal from the Lord Mayor of London. Feted as a hero in the United States, G.I. Joe lived out his days at the Detroit Zoological Gardens, where he died in 1961 at the age of 18.

G.I. Joe was the first recipient of the Dickin Medal from outside the British Commonwealth – and indeed the only one until the events of 11th September 2001.

Duke of Normandy
Pigeon NURP.41.SBC.219
Date of Award: 8 January 1947
Citation: *"For being the first bird to arrive with a message from Paratroops of 21st Army Group behind enemy lines on D Day 6 June, 1944, while serving with APS."*

Duke of Normandy was one of the many pigeons used for communication on and immediately after D-Day. He served with the 21st Army group. The soldiers he was serving with were detailed to destroy four German 110mm guns. Having successfully completed their mission, they needed to report that the guns were now out of action and, as their radios were not reliable, they turned to their pigeon. Duke of Normandy had been confined in his travelling cage for four days, and when the signaller attached the message to his leg and released him he was disorientated enough to stagger about for a few minutes and then set off in the wrong direction! Fortunately, however, he soon got his bearings and the soldiers heaved a sigh of relief as he winged his way back to base with another message vital to the conduct of the operation. The information he carried enabled support to be provided to the soldiers he had served with, saving them from enemy reprisals.

Pigeon NURP.43.CC.1418
Date of Award: 8 January 1947
Citation: *"For the fastest flight with message from 6th Airborne Div. Normandy, 7 June, 1944, while serving with APS."*

This bird was the only pigeon to make the flight home from the D-Day landings in under 24 hours (23 hours 4 minutes). Sadly her award was posthumous – this record-breaking pigeon disappeared during a subsequent flight.

Pigeon DD.43.T.139 (Australian Army Signal Corps)
Date of award: February 1947
Citation: *"During a heavy tropical storm this bird was released from Army Boat 1402 which had foundered on Wadou Beach in the Huon Gulf. Homing 40 miles to Madang it brought a message which enabled a rescue ship to be sent in time to salvage the craft and its valuable cargo of stores and ammunition."*

A blue bar cock from the Australian Pigeon Section, he was attached to Detachment 55 Port Craft Company, based at Madang, on the north coast of Papua New Guinea. On 12th July

1945 he was stationed aboard a supply ship which got into difficulties in a typhoon. The pigeon was sent off with an urgent message reading, 'Engine failed washed on Wadou Beach owing to heavy seas. Send help immediately. Craft rapidly filling with sand'. The brave bird battled through the storm, homing to Madang through heavy rain, covering 40 miles in 50 minutes. Successfully delivering his message, he brought help to the stricken ship and saved its vital cargo. In all, he flew a total of 23 operations, totalling 1,004 miles.

He may have been awarded the Dickin Medal, but it appears his unsentimental Australian keepers did not regard him highly enough to give him a name! Stuffed and mounted, he now resides in the Australian War Memorial.

Pigeon DD.43.Q.879 (Australian Army Signal Corps)
Date of award: February 1947
Citation: *"During an attack by Japanese on a US Marine patrol on Manus Island, pigeons were released to warn headquarters of an impending enemy counter-attack. Two were shot down but DD43 despite heavy fire directed at it reached HQ with the result that enemy concentrations were bombed and the patrol extricated."*

Another nameless Aussie, this blue chequer cock, bred and donated by A.J. Flavell of Elwood, Victoria, was with the Australian Pigeon Section and was attached to the US forces on Manus Island in the Admiralty Islands off Papua New Guinea. On 5th April 1944 he was with a patrol who came under heavy fire from the Japanese. Pinned down in dense jungle and with no other means of communication at their disposal, the patrol sent off several pigeons, which themselves came under fire from the enemy. Our hero escaped unscathed and carried his message to his base, thereby bringing relief to his patrol.

The bodies of the two Australian Dickin Medal recipients (stuffed, one hopes) were repatriated in 1945, prompting the *Sydney Sun* to eulogise:

> *Now fare you well my faithful bird,*
> *In war you were a wizard.*
> *So now your country honours you*
> *By taking out your gizzard.*

Sometimes you just have to love the Australians!

Cologne

Pigeon NURP39.NPS.144
Date of Award: unknown
Citation: *"For homing from a crashed aircraft over Cologne although seriously wounded, while serving with the RAF in 1943."*

Cologne, a red cock, had flown on over a hundred bomber operations when his bomber went missing during a raid on Cologne on 29th June 1943. Nothing was heard of the aircraft or its crew. On 16th July the pigeon made it home to his loft; he had severe injuries including a broken breastbone which had healed and over which the damaged feathers had regrown, indicating that the injuries had been sustained at the time of the sortie. A pigeon's big flight muscles are attached to the breastbone, so this injury would have been completely disabling. As soon as his wounds had healed sufficiently to enable him to fly, however, he completed his mission.

They Also Serve

Chapter 7
SIMON'S STORY

Early in 1948 HMS *Amethyst*, based in Hong Kong, returned to her home port from operations in Malaya and put into Stonecutters Island for supplies. 17-year-old Ordinary Seaman George Hickinbottom was ashore from the ship when he came upon a young cat on the dock. The little cat looked at him, as if considering whether he might be good for a meal and perhaps somewhere to sleep; the Stonecutters Island cats had a long history of becoming ships' cats, and George decided that this particular pathetic specimen would be a worthwhile addition to HMS *Amethyst*'s crew. Tucking the cat under his tunic, he sauntered innocently past the watch and carried his new crewmate to his own cramped quarters.

Luckily for Simon, the captain, Lt Cdr Ian Griffiths, liked cats; he was used to them in civilian life, and had had a ships' cat on a previous command, so he knew how useful they could be in controlling rats. Rats were always a problem on ships; not only did they eat foodstores, but they were a source of disease, particularly in the tropics. Putting on a stern face for George's benefit, Capt Griffiths warned him that if Simon left any mess on board he, George, would be up on a charge, and appointed Simon official ship's cat. There was already a dog on board, a terrier called Peggy; there is no record of Simon's relationship with Peggy, but from all we know of him he was quite capable of holding his own against a mere terrier.

There followed a very happy time for Simon. He explored the ship from stem to stern, from bridge to bilges, and entered enthusiastically upon his chosen career of ratter. He was popular with the whole crew, who spoilt him outrageously in the way of titbits, but his particular friends remained George Hickinbottom and the captain. He had a distressing habit of proudly bringing dead rats to the captain's cabin, but Capt Griffiths forgave him this little foible. When the captain set out on his evening rounds he would whistle for Simon and the two of them would inspect the ship together. Off-duty, Simon either slummed it in George's room or repaired to the captain's cabin, where he would curl up in the captain's smart gold-braided cap and go to sleep.

In December of that year, Capt Griffiths was given a new command; fortunately the new commander, Capt Bernard Skinner, was fond of cats too and, although Simon never became as close to him as he had been to Capt Griffiths, he soon settled to life with the new captain.

In April of 1949 orders came through for HMS *Amethyst* to proceed up the Yangtze River to Nanking, where HMS *Consort* was standing by in case the communist insurgents captured the city and the staff of the British Embassy there had to be evacuated. *Amethyst* was to relieve *Consort*. Britain had not taken sides in the war between the Nationalists and the Communists, but the situation was regarded as highly volatile. Conspicuously displaying both the White Ensign and the Union Jack, *Amethyst* set off cautiously up the river from Shanghai on 20th April 1949.

They had covered about a hundred miles upriver when without warning they came under fire from shore batteries manned by communist insurgents. Dodging the bombardment they carried on, but an hour or so later they came within range of another battery on the north shore, and this time they were not so lucky. Shells crashed into the wheelhouse and the bridge and in the confusion that followed *Amethyst* ran onto a mudbank. Trapped and helpless, she lay in plain view in the river. The guns of the shore battery continued to pound her, inflicting further damage. Capt Skinner was fatally wounded – he died the following day – and twenty-five of his crew were killed or seriously injured. Simon was in the captain's cabin when a shell exploded close by, blowing a huge hole in the bulkhead. Hit in the leg and back by flying shrapnel, he fled, dazed and bleeding, and found a hidden corner to lie up in.

Amethyst managed to send off a signal, 'Under heavy fire, am aground, large number of casualties'. Another direct hit killed the gun crew on the fo'c'sle. It was decided to try to evacuate the wounded to the shore, but the boat was hit, killing two men. The surgeon and his assistant were both killed by a shell while administering to the wounded on the quarterdeck. Gradually the battery fell silent, but still the crew were pinned down by snipers.

Consort dashed to the rescue, returning fire and trying to take *Amethyst* under tow, but she too came under heavy fire and was driven off. For six days *Amethyst* lay on the sandbank, until finally, at dead of night, *Consort* managed to get her off; she moved up river away from the battery. Two further ships, the *Black Swan* and the *London*, tried to reach *Amethyst* but were beaten back. An RAF Sunderland flying boat managed to deliver a doctor and medical supplies, but had to leave in a hurry when it was fired on. At last British Naval Attache Lt Cdr John Kerans reached the *Amethyst* overland from Nanking and took over command from the second officer, who had commanded since the captain's death despite being badly wounded himself. Kerans began negotiations with the communists, but they were destined to drag on for months.

Simon made his way to the deck, where he was found by a petty officer, whiskers and eyebrows singed off, his back and legs caked with dried blood, weak and frightened and severely dehydrated. The petty officer took him to the sickbay; the wounded men had all been treated by this time, so the medical officer had time to look at him. He was cleaned up, his burns were dressed and his shrapnel wounds stitched up. Privately the medical officer thought his case was hopeless; but Simon was made of stern stuff, and gradually, as he reclined at leisure in a corner of the petty officers' mess, his wounds began to heal and he began to stagger about. Sadly Lt Cdr Kerans was not a cat lover, besides being a man with a lot on his mind; when Simon turned up in his cabin, looking for his old master, and curled up in Kerans's cap he was not best pleased, and turfed the convalescent out.

Simon began to resume his ratting duties. The shelling had disturbed the rats and driven them out of their hiding places in the depths of the hull, and while Simon had been *hors de combat* they had flourished and were spreading all over the ship, making serious inroads into the precious stores and even invading the living quarters. Simon's return to duty was a great relief; he was catching at least a rat a day, to the general admiration and delight of the crew. He also found a new role, as hospital visitor to shell-shocked and traumatised sailors, lying on their bunks in the sick-bay and purring encouragingly. The medical officer was pleased to see that the men responded well to his presence; his own experiences and wounds obviously helped them to relate to him, and his indomitable courage helped them to recover from their own trauma.

All this time Simon was plotting how to win over the prickly new captain. He tried presenting him with a dead rat – after all, it had worked in the past – and Kerans, mindful of the sterling work Simon was doing among the rodent population, gave him a tentative stroke and had the courtesy to wait until Simon was out of sight before, with a shudder, throwing the offering overboard. Then he fell ill and was confined to bed for a few days and Simon, seizing his opportunity, hopped up onto his bunk and settled down to purr and knead his paws, a therapy which had cured all those sailors in the sick-bay and so was guaranteed to work on the captain. Kerans let him stay. And from then on he slept where he wanted – including in the captain's cabin.

There was one particularly large and vicious rat that was causing serious damage to the dwindling supplies. The crew nicknamed him 'Mao Tse-tung'. The men tried to trap him, and tried to steer Simon away from him; they thought poor Simon, still weakened by his ordeal, would be no match for such a fearsome creature. They could have saved themselves the trouble; Simon met the monster one day and without hesitation threw himself at the rat and killed him. He was hailed as a hero for that exploit, and promoted to the rank of Able Seacat.

The negotiations with the communists dragged on and still *Amethyst* lay in the river. Shipboard life became hot and difficult – and boring. The heat was fierce, and supplies of everything, including fuel, were running low. Often the boilers had to be shut down to save fuel, leaving the ship with no ventilation or refrigeration. Spirits flagged all over the ship. Simon continued his endless round of ratting duties, and helped the terrier Peggy with the task of keeping up the crew's morale. He rode out a typhoon sleeping peacefully in the captain's cabin. The wait wore on, with no end in sight.

Finally Lt Cdr Kerans decided to make a run for it; on 31st July, at dead of night, *Amethyst* slipped her anchor and began a 104-mile dash for the open sea, running the gauntlet of communist guns on both banks of the river. Laying down heavy black smoke to obscure her passage as dawn broke, the battered ship, at full speed ahead, broke through the boom at the mouth of the Yangtze and, after 101 days, her ordeal was over. She had lost 25 men, including her captain; nine were killed on the *Consort*, twelve on the *London*.

They Also Serve

The news of the 'Yangtze Incident' spread around the world, and by the time the ship docked in Hong Kong the crew – and Simon – were heroes. Simon and Peggy were both awarded the *Amethyst* campaign ribbon at a presentation ceremony held at the Hong Kong China Fleet Club, and Lt Cdr Kerans immediately put Simon forward for the Dickin Medal, writing the recommendation himself. 'The large number of rats on board the ship represented a real menace to the health of the ship's company,' he wrote. 'Simon rose nobly to the occasion and after two months the number of rats had diminished greatly. Throughout the incident Simon's behaviour was of the highest order.' He also noted that 'Simon's presence on the ship, together with Peggy the dog, was a decided factor in maintaining the high level of morale of the ship's company. They gave the ship an air of domesticity and normality in a situation which in other aspects was very trying.'

'Very trying'; a classic example of British understatement.

The award was confirmed on 10th August. Simon was the first – and so far the only – cat to be awarded the Medal, and the first representative of the Royal Navy.

Simon quickly became a celebrity; in the aftermath of the Second World War Britain yearned for heroes and happy endings, and the media were delighted to oblige. Photoshoots, newsreel films and a limitless quantity of purple prose carried his fame around the world, and Simon was inundated with letters, effusive poems, toys and gifts of catfood. A 'cat officer', Stuart Hett, had to be appointed to deal with his fan mail. Simon, however, modelled his demeanour on Greta Garbo and shunned the publicity. As *Amethyst* steamed home Simon turned his back on photographers and adoring fans from Singapore to Gibraltar.

His exulted status, however, did not get him out of the statutory six months in quarantine on his arrival in Britain at the beginning of November. He was ensconced in a quarantine facility in Surrey with every luxury possible and plenty of devoted attention, as well as regular visits from his *Amethyst* shipmates, and settled down to wait out his term until Lt Cdr Kerans, who had promised him a new home in civilian life, could collect him. His Dickin Medal presentation was scheduled for 11th December, and was to be attended by Maria Dickin herself as well as the Lord Mayor of London.

But it quickly became apparent that Simon was not well; a vet was sent for immediately and found he had a high temperature. Acute enteritis was diagnosed; he was given an injection and tablets, but to no avail. He sank into a final sleep, and died in the early morning of 28th November. Still a young cat, his combat experiences had weakened him and left him unable to fight off the virus. His shipmates were distraught, and the public reacted with an outpouring of cards, letters and flowers. *Time* magazine published his obituary.

Simon, borne by his shipmates to his grave in a Union Jack draped coffin, was buried in the PDSA's cemetery at Ilford with full Naval honours. His epitaph reads:

IN
MEMORY OF
"SIMON"
SERVED IN
H.M.S. AMETHYST
MAY 1948 — SEPTEMBER 1949
AWARDED DICKIN MEDAL
AUGUST 1949
DIED 28TH NOVEMBER 1949.
THROUGHOUT THE YANGTZE INCIDENT
HIS BEHAVIOUR WAS OF THE HIGHEST ORDER

Chapter 8
AND STILL THEY SERVE

Fifty-four Dickin Medals were awarded between 1943 and 1949, and then for fifty years there were no more.

And yet there are still wars, and wherever men and women fight they will be accompanied by their loyal animal comrades.

Since 2000, eleven Dickin Medals have been awarded, all to dogs. Of these, two were belated awards for deeds of gallantry performed in the Second World War and the Malayan troubles of the early 1950s; three were awarded to dogs who had displayed exceptional valour in the terrorist attacks in New York and Washington D.C. on 11th September 2001; and six have been awarded to dogs serving with the British Army in conflicts all over the world. Five of these were explosives sniffer dogs.

'It costs over £30,000 to train each one of these dogs,' Major Chris Ham of the Royal Army Veterinary Corps has pointed out, 'which is more than worth it when you consider the amount of lives that are saved each time this dog successfully finds another explosive device.

'Technology is getting better at detecting these devices, but there is nothing better than a dog's nose – that's a fact.

'The Royal Army Veterinary Corps is the only area of the army which is expanding, which in itself shows you how important these dogs are.'

The Forgotten Heroes

Gander – Newfoundland

Date of Award: awarded posthumously on 27 October 2000
Citation: *"For saving the lives of Canadian infantrymen during the Battle of Lye Mun on Hong Kong Island in December 1941. On three documented occasions Gander, the Newfoundland mascot of the Royal Rifles of Canada engaged the enemy as his regiment joined the Winnipeg Grenadiers, members of Battalion Headquarters 'C' Force and other Commonwealth troops in their courageous defence of the Island. Twice Gander's attacks halted the enemy's advance and protected groups of wounded soldiers. In a final act of bravery the war dog was killed in action gathering a grenade. Without Gander's intervention many more lives would have been lost in the assault."*

Newfoundland dogs are famous for their friendliness and loyalty, and many stories are told of rescues performed by these gentle giants (Newfoundlands can grow to 130–140 pounds). But there is one Newfoundland that showed bravery and devotion even beyond the breed's normal level. His name was Gander and he lost his life protecting Canadian and other Commonwealth soldiers on the beaches of Hong Kong Island during the Second World War.

In 1940, Gander (then called Pal) was the family pet of Rod Hayden, and lived on the airfield at Gander in Newfoundland. The first refuelling vehicle at Gander's airport was a 45-gallon drum lashed to a sled and towed to waiting aircraft by Pal! He was well known around the airfield and in the town – pilots landing at the airfield sometimes mistook him for a bear – and was much loved by the neighbourhood children, romping with them in the summer and towing their sleds during winter.

One day, delightedly greeting a group of his young friends, he accidentally scratched a six-year-old. Mr Hayden decided the big, friendly dog was too enthusiastic to be safe with small children; afraid he would have to put him down or, nearly as bad, curtail his freedom, he decided to present the dog to the 1st Battalion of the Royal Rifles of Canada as a mascot. Pal's new owners were delighted, and re-named him Gander in honour of his home town and as reminder of what they were all fighting for, and promoted him to Sergeant – even sewing sergeant's stripes onto his collar.

Gander and the Royal Rifles were sent to join other Commonwealth troops on Hong Kong Island in October 1941, to defend the island against attacks by the Japanese. During the

Battle of Lye Mun, Gander displayed great bravery protecting his battalion. When the Japanese landed near the Canadian section of the beach, Gander rushed at the enemy, barking furiously and biting at their legs. On another occasion he defended a group of wounded Canadian soldiers from advancing Japanese troops, again dashing at them, barking and threatening. For some reason, instead of shooting him, the Japanese turned aside and went a different way, and the lives of the wounded soldiers were saved.

Gander's last and greatest act of courage came during yet another Japanese attack. In the heat of the fighting, an enemy grenade landed near a group of Canadian soldiers, some of them wounded. Gander knew about grenades – he had encountered them before, and if he was not aware of their deadly potential he at least knew all about the flash and the loud bang, and knew that the men were afraid of them. There can be no question but that he knew he was putting himself in danger when he snatched up the grenade in his mouth and ran off, carrying it away from the men. Some people may see this as a dog's natural instinct to 'fetch' – but if this had been a game to him, he would have carried his prize back to his friends for them to throw it again for him. No, he was undoubtedly carrying the grenade *away* from his friends to save them from the explosion he knew they feared. Tragically the grenade blew up in Gander's mouth, killing him instantly. He had given his life saving the lives of the Canadian soldiers.

Hong Kong ultimately fell, of course, and Gander's soldier friends spent the rest of the war as POWs, in soul-destroying conditions. They held onto the story about their brave dog, his memory keeping their spirits up

Over the years, the story of Gander's bravery, once well-known and told over and over in his home town, was almost forgotten. And then in the 1990s in a conversation between local historian Frank Tibbo and Mrs Eileen Elms, who as a child had known the dog as Pal, Gander's heroism was mentioned. Through their efforts, Gander's story was revived; finally, nearly sixty years after his death, he was awarded a posthumous Dickin medal, the only Canadian dog to be so recognised.

In 2015 a statue of Gander, and of a soldier of the period, was unveiled in Gander Heritage Park. 'It's very emotional, even talking about it, it's very close to my heart,' said Philip Doddridge, a member of the Royal Rifles who fought alongside Sergeant Gander and spent three years in a Japanese POW camp.

'He was very much loved by all of us, he followed us to Hong Kong and was killed in action.'

Lucky – German Shepherd

RAF number 3610 AD: RAF Police anti-terrorist tracker dog – from 1949 to 1952 during the Malaya Campaign

Date of Award: 6 February 2007

Citation: *"For the outstanding gallantry and devotion to duty of the RAF Police anti-terrorist tracker dog team, comprising Bobbie, Jasper, Lassie and Lucky, while attached to the Civil Police and several British Army regiments including the Coldstream Guards, 2nd Battalion Royal Scots Guards and the Ghurkhas during the Malaya Campaign. Bobbie, Jasper, Lassie and Lucky displayed exceptional determination and life-saving skills during the Malaya Campaign. The dogs and their handlers were an exceptional team, capable of tracking and locating the enemy by scent despite unrelenting heat and an almost impregnable jungle. Sadly, three of the dogs lost their lives in the line of duty: only Lucky survived to the end of the conflict."*

Unusually, Lucky's citation makes it clear that he received his award not only for his own bravery but on behalf of his three comrades.

In 1949 Corporal Bevel Austin Stapleton (known as Bev), an RAF Police Dog Handler, was teamed up with 3610 Air Dog Lucky, a German Shepherd, and they became inseparable. Bev and Lucky, along with Corporal Thackray, Bobbie, Lassie and Jasper, operated in the dense and steamy jungles of Malaya during the terrorist uprising from 1949-1952, tracking communist insurgents in extraordinarily difficult and dangerous conditions. The job would have been impossible without dogs; in the thick jungle the insurgents could have simply struck and melted away into the forest, invisible within a few yards. Only tracker dogs could follow and stay on their trail. The terrorists, of course, knew this, so getting rid of the dogs was a high priority. Lucky was in fact the only one of the four to survive the conflict.

On 21st January 1950, Corporals Stapleton and Thackray and their dogs were called out to help in the search for a wounded terrorist who had escaped into an area of swamp. As they hunted the area two of the dogs, Bobbie and Lassie, jumped into a pool. Bobbie just disappeared below the surface; Lassie went into violent convulsions, biting at her own back, and then sank below the water. Bev Stapleton noticed that there were dead fish floating on the surface; then he saw a cable running into the water. A live electric cable had been severed by a bullet and dropped into the water. Bobbie and Lassie had been instantly killed by the 30,000-volt current. Their deaths saved their handlers and other members of the patrol from electrocution.

One day Bev and Lucky were ambushed by a Malay gunner and a fierce firefight broke out. Lucky was deafened by the tremendous noise of the guns, but that was not enough to stop him tracking down the insurgent through thick jungle. During the campaign the determination and jungle tracking skills of the dogs were instrumental in the capture of many communist terrorists including, in 1951, Lang-Jan-Sang, a notorious gang leader responsible for the deaths of many local people. His capture prevented further casualties.

As the conflict wore on Jasper too was lost, killed in action. Only Lucky was left of his unit. He and Bev carried out several more missions, facing the dangers of both enemy action and the jungle itself, until in 1952 Bev finished his tour of duty and returned home. He retired as a Warrant Officer after 36 years' service. Lucky was assigned to another handler, though his 'jungle-beating' days were over.

Accepting the Dickin Medal on Lucky's behalf, Cpl Stapleton said, 'I've never been told what happened to him, but it doesn't matter, we were there to do a job and we just got on with it. In those days, it was just a matter of doing your job. Lucky would have understood that. He just got things done.'

9/11

As the 21st century dawned the nature of war changed forever as a well-organised and ruthlessly-executed act of terrorism brought unprecedented horror to the United States. Terrorists hijacked four civilian airliners full of passengers; two were deliberately flown into the twin towers of the World Trade Center in New York, one into the Pentagon in Washington DC, while the third crashed in Pennslyvania following a brave attempt by the passengers to regain control from the terrorists.

Within hours of the attack on the World Trade Center on 11th September 2001, specially-trained Search and Rescue (SAR) dogs were on the scene. In the days and weeks to come over 300 dogs were mobilized across the United States and Canada to join New York Police Department canine units in the round-the-clock searches of the 16-acre disaster site.

The dogs were a vital element in the search operation. Their skills and ability enabled the rescue workers to focus their efforts, covering as much ground as swiftly and yet as thoroughly as possible; and their confidence and surefooted assurance as they moved through the devastation of the debris field lessened the risk for the human searchers. Many of the handlers reported, as well, that the dogs' presence brought great comfort to the men and women of the Police and Fire Departments, searching the wreckage for the remains of colleagues killed in the line of duty on 11th September.

A mobile veterinary treatment unit provided by Suffolk County SPCA was staffed by volunteer veterinary surgeons and vet technicians. Most of the problems they dealt with were minor injuries, burns and cut paws, and dogs had their noses and eyes washed and paws cleaned and were given shots. No dogs died in the recovery effort, though a New York Port Authority bomb-sniffing dog named Sirius, who was stationed at the World Trade Center, died when the towers collapsed.

Three Dickin Medals were awarded to dogs who were involved in that terrible day and its aftermath. Two guide dogs, Roselle and Salty, saved their owners from high up in the stricken towers; and New York Police dog Appollo received his medal as representative of all the SAR dogs who served so conscientiously.

Salty and Roselle – Labrador Guide dogs

Date of Award: 5 March 2002
Citation: *"For remaining loyally at the side of their blind owners, courageously leading them down more than 70 floors of the World Trade Center and to a place of safety following the terrorist attack on New York on 11 September 2001."*

Salty and Roselle's stories are told in chapter 9.

Appollo – German Shepherd

Date of Award: 5 March 2002
(NYPD dog Appollo received the PDSA Dickin Medal on behalf of all the Search and Rescue dogs at Ground Zero and the Pentagon following the terrorist attack on 11th September 2001.)
Citation: *"For tireless courage in the service of humanity during the search and rescue operations in New York and Washington on and after 11 September 2001. Faithful to words of command and undaunted by the task, the dogs' work and unstinting devotion to duty stand as a testament to those lost or injured."*

Appollo was chosen by the New York Police Department to receive the Dickin Medal on behalf of all the Search and Rescue dogs involved in the aftermath of the attacks on the World Trade Center and on the Pentagon in Washington D.C.

10-year-old German Shepherd Appollo had been in the NYPD K-9 unit since 1994 and, trained for gun recovery, urban search and rescue, and cadaver searching, was one of their top dogs. Like all members of the K-9 unit, he lived with his handler, Police Officer Peter Davis, who had custody of him 24 hours a day, at home and at work. They had built a close friendship and had an impressive record in the line of duty.

11th September began as a normal day for Officer Davis and Appollo, but when the call came they were sent straight to the World Trade Centre, where Appollo was the first rescue dog on the scene, just 15 minutes after the second tower collapsed. The scene was one of unimaginable devastation. To get to the site of the towers they had to clamber over and around rubble; at times Officer Davis was wading through knee-deep water, while Appollo had to swim.

Suddenly there was a roar and a heap of debris came crashing down, sending dust and flames into the air. Appollo disappeared. Officer Davis and a colleague ran to the spot where they had last seen him; down in a pit in the rubble, surrounded by fire, they saw the dog. Desperately they reached in and pulled him clear, his coat singed, burning embers lodged in the fur. Only the fact that he was soaking wet, having swum and splashed through the standing water on the way in, saved him. The two officers brushed the smouldering embers from his coat and, with a quick pat and a word of encouragement, he was ready to return to his work.

More than 300 Search and Rescue dog teams (dog and handler) served at Ground Zero and the Pentagon. In New York the teams were coordinated by Suffolk County SPCA, who also provided the mobile veterinary units that gave veterinary care to the rescue dogs and the thousands of injured pets. In Washington the teams were provided by the Federal Emergency Management Agency (FEMA). Teams came from all over the United States and beyond; over 70 organizations sent teams and many volunteers simply turned up to help.

All 300 dogs and their handlers went through hell as they worked in physically demanding and emotionally draining conditions. The humans had some sense of the absolute enormity of what had happened to spur them on; but the dogs worked with a single-minded dedication that came entirely from within themselves. Even when it became clear that all chance of finding survivors was gone, dogs and handlers searched on. The persistence and determination of the dogs was remarkable, astonishing even to their own handlers. Day after day they were 'flown' into the heart of the debris field in baskets slung on cables, day after day they were brought out exhausted, often with cut and grazed paws, but they never gave up. If they seemed disheartened by the hopeless search, a volunteer hid in the rubble to be found alive and 'rescued' and the dog would return to the operation with restored zeal.

Nominating one dog from among all the 300 to receive the award was almost impossible. Finally it was decided that it should be an NYPD dog as they were the first on the scene at Ground Zero and the last remaining as the operation wound down. NYPD themselves selected Appollo. With his distinguished career to date, first on the scene, going to work with his coat singed and smouldering – an outstanding candidate, and yet an equal comrade to all the other brave dogs who worked tirelessly to locate survivors and, when all hope was gone, to find remains and perhaps bring a little peace to those who had lost loved ones.

Appollo was awarded the Dickin Medal on behalf of all the search and rescue teams at Ground Zero and the Pentagon 'for tireless courage in the service of humanity'.

Into the new millennium

Sam – German Shepherd
Royal Army Veterinary Corps
Date of Award: 14 January 2003
Citation: *"For outstanding gallantry in April 1998, while assigned to the Royal Canadian Regiment in Drvar during the conflict in Bosnia-Hertzegovina. On two documented occasions Sam displayed great courage and devotion to duty. On 18 April Sam successfully brought down an armed man threatening the lives of civilians and Service personnel. On 24 April, while guarding a compound harbouring Serbian refugees, Sam's determined approach held off rioters until reinforcements arrived. This dog's true valour saved the lives of many servicemen and civilians during this time of human conflict."*

Sam served with the Royal Army Veterinary Corps (RAVC) Dog Unit. In 1998 British troops were deployed as part of an international peacekeeping force in Bosnia-Herzegovina; with his handler, Sgt Iain Carnegie, Sam was sent to the town of Drvar, which had been the scene of horrific violence just three years before, when some 17,000 ethnic Serbs had been massacred. Now an uneasy peace prevailed; Iain and Sam patrolled the streets of the little town, hoping to keep it that way.

On one of their patrols trouble erupted suddenly, when a gunman opened fire. As he fled, Sam gave chase, successfully bringing down the suspect and holding him until Iain arrived to disarm him, relieving him of a loaded pistol.

'Sam performed brilliantly,' said Iain, 'just like a training exercise.'

Six days later a potentially lethal situation arose when a furious Bosnian Muslim mob armed with crowbars, makeshift clubs and stones surrounded a group of about fifty Serbs who had taken refuge in a warehouse.

Sam and Iain went to the rescue, guarding the main entrance, facing a hail of rocks. The mob tried again and again to break in, but Sam, though he had sustained several injuries in the melee, repeatedly chased them off. Without his indomitable devotion to duty the besieged civilians would almost certainly have been killed.

'Sam displayed outstanding courage in the face of the rioters,' Iain said. 'Not once did he shy away.' Reinforcements eventually arrived, and the mob was dispersed. Iain Carnegie won a mention in dispatches for the incident; Sam, who died of natural causes two years later at the age of 10, would posthumously be awarded the Dickin Medal.

Iain said, 'I could never have attempted to carry out my duties without Sam. His true valour undoubtedly saved the lives of many servicemen and civilians.'

RAVC spokesman Lt Col Gerald Dineley agreed: 'Sam upheld the very best traditions of British army dogs. He was a wonderful and loyal servant to his handler.'

Buster – Springer Spaniel
Royal Army Veterinary Corps
Date of Award: 9 December 2003
Citation: *"For outstanding gallantry in March 2003 while assigned to the Duke of Wellington's Regiment in Safwan, Southern Iraq. Arms and explosives search dog Buster located an arsenal of weapons and explosives hidden behind a false wall in a property linked with an extremist group. Buster is considered responsible for saving the lives of service personnel and civilians. Following the find, all attacks ceased and shortly afterwards troops replaced their steel helmets with berets."*

During March 2003 in the town of Safwan, southern Iraq, British troops were bogged down as the enemy melted into the civilian population. Local people were fearful of Fedayeen fighters and Baath party separatists, who were armed and posing a severe danger to soldiers and civilians. The troops were experiencing random bomb and rocket grenade attacks and sporadic sniper fire; intelligence reports indicated a group of houses as the headquarters of extremists responsible for the attacks.

On 31st March, 200 troops of the Duke of Wellington's Regiment carried out a dawn raid against the houses, supported by armour from the Queen's Dragoon Guards. Sixteen people were arrested, but they denied any knowledge of arms or explosives. A thorough search was made without success, but the troops remained convinced that there were weapons concealed in the premises. So dog handler Sgt Danny Morgan unleashed Buster, a specially-trained explosives sniffer dog.

Buster, a five-year-old Springer spaniel, had been recruited into the Royal Army Veterinary Corps from a rehoming centre. He joined the Morgan household, becoming a firm favourite with Danny's wife and his little daughter. Danny trained Buster by teaching him to fetch guns and ammunition instead of sticks and balls.

Regulations require that the dog always goes first in case there are booby traps, and Danny had an anxious wait as Buster started his search. Suddenly the dog became very excited, and his handler knew he had found something. First he located a pistol and ammunition, and then, in a cavity in the wall, covered with a sheet of tin and with a wardrobe pushed up against it, a veritable arsenal of weapons and explosives. The haul included AK47 assault rifles, a pistol, primed grenades, grenade fuses, ammunition in magazines, loose ammunition, bomb making equipment and large quantities of cash, drugs and propaganda material.

Following the find, all attacks ceased and shortly afterwards troops replaced their steel helmets with berets. Buster is considered responsible for saving the lives of countless troops and civilians and for preventing untold misery for thousands of people, should the arms and drugs have been used or put into circulation. The discovery was credited, in effect, with ending the southern insurgency

'We'd never have found the weapons without him and they would still be a threat to our troops and the local population,' Danny said. 'I'm very proud of him.' Describing Buster as his 'best friend', he said ruefully that his little daughter had been upset when he went off to war – but had wept buckets when saying goodbye to Buster.

Buster, one of 20 or so dogs who saw service in Iraq, was so valuable to the army that he even had his own protective gear in case of chemical or biological attack. When missile or gas attack warnings sounded, he jumped into a special sealed pen equipped with an electric motor to pump air through a gas mask filter.

Sadie – Labrador

RAVC arms and explosive search dog – Kabul, Afghanistan in November 2005

Date of Award: 6 February 2007

Citation: *"For outstanding gallantry and devotion to duty while assigned to the Royal Gloucestershire, Berkshire and Wiltshire Light Infantry during conflict in Afghanistan in 2005. On 14 November 2005 military personnel serving with NATO's International Security Assistance Force in Kabul were involved in two separate attacks. Sadie and Lance Corporal Yardley were deployed to search for secondary explosive devices.*

Sadie gave a positive indication near a concrete blast wall and multinational personnel were moved to a safe distance. Despite the obvious danger Sadie and Lance Corporal Yardley completed their search. At the site of Sadie's indication, bomb disposal operators later made safe an explosive device. The bomb was designed to inflict maximum injury. Sadie's actions undoubtedly saved the lives of many civilians and soldiers."

Sadie, a nine-year-old black Labrador, was a war veteran who had already served in Iraq, Bosnia and Kosovo when she was posted to Kabul in Afghanistan with her handler Lance Corporal Karen Yardley.

As a trained explosives sniffer dog, Sadie was called in after suicide bombers had driven a bus into a German army convoy outside the United Nations headquarters, killing one soldier. The insurgents in Afghanistan often planted secondary devices in the vicinity that would be detonated by troops following up from the first explosion, so the area had to be thoroughly searched before the incident could be considered over.

Within minutes Sadie had found something. She froze, quivering; Karen immediately evacuated the area and the bomb disposal experts went in. Hidden behind a two-foot-thick concrete blast wall inside the compound they found a deadly booby-trap – a innocent-looking pressure cooker packed full of high explosives. There were over 200 people within range of the bomb, including British, American, German and Greek soldiers; the bombers had intended to massacre large numbers of soldiers and civilians – but Sadie thwarted the plot by discovering the bomb.

Karen said, 'Had Sadie not found the secondary bomb, scores of lives would have been lost. It would have exploded, killing and injuring both through the blast and through fragments. This is the sort of job that would take a patrol of soldiers several hours to do, but Sadie was able to do it in a matter of minutes.'

Treo – Labrador
Royal Army Veterinary Corps
Date of Award: 24 February 2010
Citation: *"In March 2008, Treo was deployed to Helmand Province, Afghanistan, to search for weapons and munitions concealed by the Taliban. On 15 August, while acting as forward protection for 8 Platoon, The Royal Irish Regiment, Treo located an improvised explosive device on a roadside where soldiers were about to pass. On 3 and 4 September, Treo's actions detected a further device, saving 7 Platoon from guaranteed casualties. Without doubt, Treo's actions and devotion to his duties, while in the throes of conflict, saved many lives."*

Unusually for a black Labrador, two-year-old Treo was bad-tempered and badly-behaved – so much so that his owners considered having him put down before finally deciding to hand him to the Army for training. He responded well to Army discipline and took to his new work as an explosives-sniffer. He was based in Northern Ireland when he was introduced to his new handler, Sgt Dave Heyhoe – and, in Dave's words, it was 'love at first sight'.

In 2008 Dave and Treo were attached to 104 Military Working Dog Support Unit, Royal Army Veterinary Corps, in Afghanistan. He quickly proved his worth: on his first patrol he found a hoard of weapons hidden in a mud-walled compound. In March 2008, while working as a 'forward detection dog' in Sangin he found a 'daisy chain' (a string of bombs wired together and concealed at the roadside to cause maximum casualties). He obviously made an impact; the Royal Marines began intercepting enemy radio messages urging their fighters to target the 'black dog'. Clearly getting rid of Treo was an important part of the enemy's strategy.

In September he found another daisy chain, saving another platoon from guaranteed casualties. According to the Army, his actions have also saved other soldiers and civilians from death or serious injury.

It can be common practice for handlers to request another dog if they believe they've got too close to their charge but Dave said he would not swap Treo. 'You have to understand each other, recognise the slightest change in each other. The trick is to channel your fear, knowing that this will make both you and the dog concentrate better.'

Treo and Dave retired in 2009.

Theo – Springer Spaniel
Royal Army Veterinary Corps, Arms and Explosives Search dog
Date of Award: posthumously on 25 October 2012
Citation: *"For outstanding gallantry and devotion to duty while deployed with 104 Military Working Dog (MWD) Squadron during conflict in Afghanistan in September 2010 to March 2011."*

The partnership of Lance Corporal Liam Tasker and Theo, described by colleagues as 'inseparable', had been hugely successful. Theo helped uncover not only hidden explosive devices, but also the materials that could be used to make them. During one operation Theo identified two bags of fertiliser and a large quantity of parts intended to make IEDs (improvised explosive devices). On another occasion, Theo found an underground tunnel leading to a room in which insurgents were suspected of making bombs and hiding from coalition forces. In fact, the pair had uncovered 14 bombs and hoards of weapons in five months in Helmand Province – more than any other dog and handler in the conflict.

On 1st March 2011, Theo and Liam were on a mission in support of the Irish Guards in the Nahr-e Saraj district of Helmand when the patrol came under enemy fire.

Liam was killed.

Theo was being taken back to base, in the care of other members of the patrol, when he started having seizures. Despite immediate first aid and veterinary treatment he died.

When the story of the dog who died of a broken heart broke, it touched the nation.

When Theo was awarded the Dickin Medal Liam's mother said, 'We are absolutely delighted and so very, very proud. It means so much because Liam put Theo forward for the medal when he was in Afghanistan because he was so good. Liam got his Mention in Dispatches [*the oldest recognition of gallantry in the Armed Forces*], so it's lovely that Theo is getting his Dickin Medal and being recognised for his bravery as well. I strongly believe that Theo died of a broken heart. I take comfort in that.'

Colonel Neil Smith, director of the Army Veterinary Service, said: 'This impressive team undoubtedly prevented many soldiers and civilians being killed or injured. This award recognises not only a very special dog, but also the contribution that all our dog teams make in detecting improvised explosive devices and weapons caches.'

Sasha – Labrador
Royal Army Veterinary Corps, Arms and Explosives Search dog
Date of Award: posthumously on 21 May 2014
Citation: *"For outstanding gallantry and devotion to duty while assigned to 2nd Battalion, The Parachute Regiment, in Afghanistan 2008."*

Lance Corporal Kenneth Rowe, 24, of the Royal Army Veterinary Corps, had been due to leave front-line duties the day before, but had persuaded his superiors to let him stay because he was worried about the lack of cover. He was on a routine patrol with his explosives sniffer-dog Sasha from their base in Sangin province when they came under enemy fire. Both Kenneth and Sasha were killed in the attack, while six soldiers from the Parachute Regiment were injured. Sasha was the first dog killed in operations in Afghanistan or Iraq. Kenneth's commanding officer, Major Stuart McDonald, praised his decision to stay on at the base and continue patrolling. 'This unselfish action epitomised his professionalism and dedication to his job,' he said.

Sasha has been credited with 15 'finds' of bombs, mortars, mines and other weapons – thought to be more than any other dog in the conflict. On one occasion she detected two mortars and a large quantity of weapons, including explosives and mines.

Commanders said Sasha had undoubtedly saved many soldiers and civilians from death or injury. Soldiers (always a more sentimental bunch than you might suppose) said her calmness, friendliness and wagging tail were comforting and reassuring.

During their time together, Kenneth and Sasha forged a unique bond, and were considered the best handler and dog team in the region. His mother later said: 'Kenneth always adored animals and loved working with his dogs. He took his role protecting his fellow soldiers very seriously. We are so proud of him, and he would be incredibly proud that Sasha's bravery is being recognised with the Dickin Medal.'

PDSA Director-General Jan McLoughlin said: 'We are extremely proud to be awarding a posthumous medal to Sasha. The award is even more poignant as we approach the centenary of World War One and are reminded of the huge debt we owe the animals who serve in times of conflict.

'Sasha's exceptional devotion to duty in Afghanistan saved many lives, both soldiers and civilians. This medal honours Sasha's unwavering service and her ultimate sacrifice.'

Chapter 9
SALTY AND ROSELLE'S STORIES

11th September 2001 started like any other morning at the World Trade Center in New York City. By the start of the working day around fifteen thousand people were in the offices and restaurants of the two tall 110-storey towers. Unknown to them, dramatic events were unfolding in the skies above them.

On that fateful morning, terrorists had seized control of four aeroplanes: American Airlines Flight 11 and United Airlines Flight 175, both en route from Boston to Los Angeles; American Airlines Flight 77 from Washington DC to Los Angeles; and United Airlines Flight 93 from Newark, New Jersey, to San Francisco. Two of these planes were now heading for New York.

At 8.46 am Flight 11 was crashed into the World Trade Center's North Tower, between the 93rd and 99th floors; a huge explosion was followed by devastating fire. Seventeen minutes later Flight 175 struck the South Tower between the 77th and 85th floors. In both towers, jet fuel exploded and, burning, cascaded down the stairwells, carrying the fire with it. Hundreds of people, including everybody aboard both planes, were killed instantly in the impacts; others were trapped above the crash floors or killed when the buildings collapsed. The South Tower collapsed at 9.59 am, and the North Tower at 10.28 am. In all, nearly three thousand people lost their lives in New York that day: aircraft passengers, workers in the buildings, police and firefighters. From the North Tower, into the horror and devastation of the streets below, emerged two remarkable guide dogs, devotedly leading their blind masters to safety.

Omar Rivera, originally from Colombia, was a computer technician with the Port Authority of New York and New Jersey. He had lost his sight to glaucoma at the age of 27. Like Michael Hingson, whose story follows, he refused to give in to his blindness and made himself a successful career, using a computer with voice-recognition software. On the morning of 11th September he was at his desk on the 71st floor of the North Tower of the World Trade Center, his four-year-old yellow Labrador guide dog Salty curled up under his desk, when the first hijacked airliner crashed into the tower 25 floors above him.

Omar leapt to his feet; the building was rocking and he could hear the rustling of scattered papers, the sound of broken glass flying around and crunching underfoot, the crash as his computer slid off his desk, and the screams of other workers. Salty vanished, swept away by the rush of people fleeing down the stairs, and Omar found himself on his own for several terrifying minutes amid the tumult, believing that Salty had fled. Omar was sure he was going to die – there was no way he could escape down 70 floors of destruction and hysterical crowds – but he hoped poor, frightened Salty would escape. The noise and the heat were terrifying and people were rushing past, making for the stairs. But then, to his amazement, he felt the familiar nudge of Salty's head against his knee.

A friend dashed in from across the hall and cried, 'Omar, it's time to go!' Quickly Omar clipped on Salty's lead and they began to make their way through the commotion to the stairs. 'Let's go! Let's go!' shouted the friend. Salty was very nervous, but he did not falter; calmly he led Omar out onto the congested stairway. People were screaming and shouting. Everything was streaming with water, and the air was thick with smoke and the smell of burning. 'I heard people crying, screaming, praying,' Omar recalled. 'I remember how wet everything was. And I remember the burning smells, especially the terrible smell of jet fuel. We passed many people who would not or could not continue.' The three stuck together, Omar's friend on his right and Salty on his left, leading the way.

As they descended Omar could feel the building swaying and hear the awful sounds of the walls and floors cracking and buckling around him. He was glad he couldn't see the destruction; his blindness allowed him to concentrate on the immediate goal of reaching the safety of the ground. His friend kept yelling, 'Just keep going!' and shouting out the floor numbers. Seventy... sixty... fifty... The narrow stairwell was jam-packed with frightened people, crowding and pushing past Omar and his escorts. Still Salty led on.

Gradually order began to prevail. People began to accept the inevitability of a very long and tiring descent, and they settled into a steady pace, inching down the stairway through slabs of rubble and pools of water from burst pipes. Omar could hear the groaning of the building, moving under intolerable pressure, twisting and then failing. The stairwell was full of thick smoke and the stink of jet fuel. Many people sank exhausted on the stairs, unable to carry on. Still Salty led on, floor after floor, down and down. Forty... someone, trying to be helpful, offered to take Salty's lead. Salty would have none of it. He refused to leave Omar's side. He still had a job to do. Thirty... there were people going the other way now, firefighters who were climbing upwards. Omar thought of his family and prayed that he would see them again. He thought of Salty, steadily leading him downwards; he kept thinking, 'We're a team, we go together. We're a team, we go together...' Twenty... fifteen... ten...

It took them an hour and a quarter to come down those seventy terrible floors.

As they finally staggered out into the lobby, Omar says, 'My friend yelled, "RUN!" But we couldn't. The lobby was a mess, full of debris we had to step over. People were jumping from the building and it was dangerous to get out. I held tight to Salty's leash and when we were clear of the building, we ran. We just ran! We were two or three blocks away when we heard the building falling. I knew immediately what was happening.'

They stumbled on through clouds of toxic dust and smoke, throats choked, eyes burning. Salty was exhausted and Omar was numb, only vaguely aware of the people around them, crying, screaming. People were praying; so was Omar. And a lot of people were praying for him; his family, watching events unfold on television, were desperate. It seemed impossible that a blind man could escape from that carnage. Phones were not working, and they could get no news. Transport systems were in chaos. The day dragged by, and they became more and more convinced that he was gone for ever.

But at last, thanks to the dog's courage and loyalty, Omar and Salty came home.

Michael Hingson had been blind since birth, and got his first guide dog at the age of 14. He had never allowed his blindness to interfere with his life, and by 2001 he was a highly-qualified and successful software-company executive. Roselle, the three-and-a-half-year-old yellow Labrador who accompanied him to his office on the 78th floor of the North Tower of the World Trade Center, was the fifth guide dog he had had.

When the plane struck twenty floors above Michael had no idea what had happened, but he realised it was something serious. Quickly, he told the few people in his office to get out, using the stairs – as a Californian he was familiar with evacuation procedures in the event of an earthquake, and knew elevators can fail in emergencies. He grabbed Roselle's harness and began giving her the commands that would tell her she was now on duty. But, startled out of her morning nap under his desk, she was already ready to go. Colleague David Frank hurried across to help, and he, Michael and Roselle headed for the stairs. The stairwell was already filling with frightened people as they began the long descent. As they went down, more and more people crowded out onto the stairs. There was no real panic, but people were fearful and confused, and everyone was hurrying; despite this, Roselle remained calm and focussed on her job. It also began to get hotter, with temperatures eventually rising to over 90 degrees, and the stifling air was full of the fumes of jet fuel. Soon Michael was sweating, and Roselle was panting heavily, hot, thirsty and with her throat burnt by the fumes.

By the time they got down to the 50th floor, the second plane had crashed into the South Tower, although Michael and David only learned of this much later. The fumes were thicker, catching in their throats and stinging their eyes, and people were bumping into them. Now they met the firefighters climbing up towards the inferno forty floors above. At the sight of them there was tired but heartfelt applause from the frightened people on the stairs. Several of the firefighters petted Roselle as they passed, and she licked their hands. 'It was the last act of unconditional love those firefighters got,' Michael said later.

By now temperatures in the North Tower were reaching 1,000 degrees at the top of the building, and the heat was leaking into the stairwell every time someone opened a door to join the crowds making their way down to safety. The stairs were jammed with people now, still for the most part well-disciplined, but moving as fast as they could, trying to push past David, Michael and Roselle. Michael was worried about his dog – she was panting heavily, obviously in distress, but she carried on dauntlessly, leading her master down, always down towards the safety of the ground so far below. David Frank stayed with them.

Fifty minutes after emerging onto the stairwell on the 78th floor and beginning the nightmare descent, they finally made it to the lobby. They were met with a scene of chaos; dust and debris was everywhere and burst pipes spewed water onto the floor. Roselle stopped to snatch a much-needed drink at one of the puddles and then guided her master through the confusion to the doors. They were barely out onto the street when, with an unearthly roar, the South Tower collapsed; David, Michael and Roselle started running for the subway. In all that chaos and danger, the hideous noise of the skyscraper's fall and the screams of terror all around them, Roselle stayed calm and did her job, guiding Michael unfalteringly until a police officer steered them into the subway where they could find shelter.

They ventured out after about 20 minutes and began to make their way north, only to be caught again as the North Tower collapsed in on itself, sending a billowing cloud of ash and debris racing up the street towards them. Coughing and choking, they stumbled on, even managing to lend assistance to others temporarily blinded by the dust, until finally the danger, if not the horror, was behind them.

When her world – literally – collapsed around her, Roselle remained true to her training and dedicated to her master, and brought him to safety.

The inhalation of particulates from the clouds of toxic dust eventually took its toll on Roselle, and in March 2007 she had to retire due to a blood disorder. Although her place as Michael's guide dog was taken by another, she stayed on as a family pet until her death in 2011.

'She never hesitated,' Michael says proudly of his brave companion. 'She never panicked.'

At a gala dinner a few months later Omar and Salty were presented with gold medallions by Guiding Eyes for the Blind. Salty's trainer, Caroline McCabe-Sandler, presented the awards. She said, 'We hear of animals persevering over great odds, and we hear of people persevering over great odds, but Omar's and Salty's story is that of a team, human and animal, persevering together over horrific odds.'

The same is true for Michael and Roselle, and indeed for every Dickin Medal winner.

They Also Serve

Chapter 10
LEST WE FORGET

The Dickin Medal was introduced in 1943, and was awarded a total of 54 times between 1943 and 1949 – to 32 pigeons, 18 dogs, three horses, and one cat. After a gap of nearly half a century, a further 11 – all to dogs – were awarded.

Conspicuously missing was any recognition of the animal heroes of the First World War. The Medal hadn't been available then, but of course animals, particularly the equine species, played a major role in that conflict. On all sides, eight million horses and countless mules and donkeys died. The RSPCA memorial at Kilburn commemorates the 'deaths by enemy action, disease or accident of 484,143 horses mules, camels and bullocks and of many hundreds of dogs, carrier pigeons and other creatures, on the various fronts during the Great War.'

Britain's first military action of the war was a cavalry charge, near Mons in August 1914, but cavalry was already fading into history. When the war broke out in Western Europe Britain and Germany had cavalry forces each numbering about 100,000 men, and there was a general belief in the supremacy of the cavalry attack. No-one could have contemplated the horrors of the trenches.

However, that cavalry charge near Mons was practically the last seen in the war. Trench warfare made such charges not only impractical but impossible. Machine guns, trench complexes and barbed wire effectively consigned the cavalry charge to a bygone military age.

Most of the horses of the First World War were used for transport. Cars and lorries often went wrong but horses and mules could be relied on to get food and equipment to the front line. There were packhorses, artillery teams, and horses pulling everything from heavy wagons to ambulances.

Dogs had a vital part to play in the First World War as the complexes of trenches spread throughout the Western Front. It is estimated that by 1918, Germany had employed 30,000 dogs, Britain, France and Belgian over 20,000 and Italy 3000. America, at first, did not use dogs except to utilise a few hundred from the Allies for specific missions. Later they developed their own dog service. Dogs played various roles in the First World War – guards, scouts (who went out with patrols), messengers and medical dogs.

As the centenary year of the First World War approached, there was a feeling that some recognition should be made of the animals who had fought and died in that dreadful conflict.

On 2nd September 2014 the first Honorary PDSA Dickin Medal ever presented in the charity's 97 year history ensured that all the animals that served on the front line during the First World War were duly recognised for their gallantry and devotion to duty. The chosen recipient, standing as representative for all the others, was a remarkable horse called Warrior.

WARRIOR'S STORY

Warrior, a bay gelding with a white star, arrived on the Western Front on 11th August 1914 and remained on the front line throughout the war. He was one of the lucky horses who made it back to Britain. He was also more fortunate than requisitioned horses, who went to war with strangers; he went with his owner, General Jack Seely (later Lord Mottistone). The two knew and loved each other and their bond helped them through four grim years of battle. Jack Seely had raised Warrior from a foal on the Isle of Wight.

Seely had fought in the Boer War and when war broke out in 1914 he volunteered to serve at the Front. Warrior went with him, sailing in the same ship. As a general's horse he had an easier life than many, but he still had to work hard, carrying

Seely from one post to another, reconnoitring positions, advancing and then retreating as the war ebbed and flowed. Almost immediately Warrior adapted to his new surroundings, showing no fear when shells burst nearby. Never did he attempt to bolt, even when every horse around him was killed by shells.

They saw action on the first day of the Battle of the Somme in 1916; Warrior was stuck fast in the mud when German aeroplanes flew low and strafed all the horses with their machine guns, but he was not hit. In the soul-destroying mud of Passchendaele in 1917 a huge shell fell near him and he was completely buried under earth except for one forefoot. He was dug out, none the worse for his experience.

Nowhere was safe, but Warrior was a miraculously lucky horse. Once a stable where he was sheltering was hit by six shells, but Warrior somehow escaped unhurt. Another time the horse next to him was cut clean in half by a shell, but Warrior was untouched. Dug out of the mud, twice rescued from burning stables, miraculously surviving shells and gunfire as men and horses fell around him, Warrior became known as 'the horse the Germans could not kill'.

According to records, Warrior displayed gallantry above and beyond the call of duty. He was an inspiration to the soldiers as they faced bayonets, bullets, gas and tanks. The troops liked General Seely, but they loved Warrior. Everywhere he went he was greeted and fussed over. He was more than a mascot: the General's horse with the trusting eyes had become the soldiers' friend and inspiration. When he was not working, Warrior would follow Seely around like a dog, trotting at his heels. He was greeted with shouts of 'Here comes old Warrior' wherever he went. Seely called him 'my passport', for with Warrior beneath him or beside him he was always sure of a friendly welcome. The tough Canadians of Seely's brigade immediately warmed to the gentle bay horse and, because they loved him, they loved Seely, too.

Seely observed that, despite their sufferings with the cold and mud, the rats and lice, soldiers always brightened at the sight of the horses. 'One of the finest things about that indomitable creature, the soldier of the frontline, was his invariable kindness and gentleness at all times to the horses,' wrote Seely. 'Again and again I have seen a man risk his life and, indeed, lose it, for the sake of his horse.'

In March 1918 they led the charge up the Morueil Ridge, one of the last great cavalry charges and a decisive battle in the history of the First World War. It would be led by a group of 14 men and horses, with Seely and Warrior at their head.

No sooner had Seely given the orders, than, as he remembered: 'Warrior took charge and... with a great leap, started off. All sensation of fear had vanished from him as he galloped on at racing speed. He bounded into the air as we passed our infantry.' Through a hail of bullets from the enemy they charged up the ridge towards the wood at the top. Nearly half the horses went down, but Warrior did not flinch or hesitate. On he galloped, the others thundering after him over the soft turf until they reached the trees. At once the first squadron, 80-strong, came thundering up the hill. Behind them came squadron after squadron. The hillside was pounded by hooves as men and horses raced towards the fighting.

It was a turning point — after Moreuil Wood, the German offensive faltered, and their advance was checked. The triumph was, Seely said: 'Not due to me, but to my horse Warrior. It was he who did not hesitate, did not flinch, though well he knew the danger from those swift bullets.'

Shortly after that, Warrior went lame, and Seely took another horse into battle. That horse was killed and Seely was gassed and invalided home, leaving Warrior behind in France. He begged to be allowed to return to the Front, but it was months before he was fit enough to return, and by then the war was all but over. On 11th November 1918 the Armistice was signed.

'Nearly all Warrior's comrades were killed,' wrote Seely, 'and nearly all of mine, but we both survived – largely because of him.' At a victory parade in Hyde Park, Seely's Canadian comrades-in-arms greeted their favourite horse with the shout: 'Here comes old Warrior!'

Seely and Warrior returned home to the Isle of Wight in 1918, where they rode together for many a year until the old warhorse's death in 1941, aged 33. The *Times* and the *London Evening Standard* ran obituaries of the great horse, and he was also immortalised by the famous painter Alfred Munnings who, as a war artist attached to Seely's troops, painted the magnificent Warrior on many occasions.

PDSA Director-General, Jan McLoughlin, said: 'Warrior's gallantry and devotion to duty throughout the First World War reflects the bravery shown by the millions of horses, dogs, pigeons and other animals engaged in the war. That is why he is a worthy recipient of this very special Honorary PDSA Dickin Medal – the first and only of its kind. And in this anniversary year of remembrance there can surely be no more fitting way to honour the bravery and sacrifice that millions of noble animals displayed during World War One.'

They Also Serve

They Also Serve

Appendix 1

ROLL OF HONOUR

DOGS

Bob – Mongrel
6th Royal West Kent Regt.
Date of Award: 24 March 1944
"For constant devotion to duty with special mention of Patrol work at Green Hill, North Africa while serving with 6th Battalion Queens Own Royal West Kent Regt."

Jet – Alsatian
MAP Serving with Civil Defence
Date of Award: 12 January 1945
"For being responsible for the rescue of persons trapped under blitzed buildings while serving with the Civil Defence Services of London."

Irma – Alsatian
MAP Serving with Civil Defence
Date of Award: 12 January 1945
"For being responsible for the rescue of persons trapped under blitzed buildings while serving with the Civil Defences of London."

Beauty – Wire-Haired Terrier
PDSA Rescue Squad
Date of Award: 12 January 1945
"For being the pioneer dog in locating buried air-raid victims while serving with a PDSA Rescue Squad."

Rob – Collie
War Dog No. 471/332 Special Air Service
Date of Award: 22 January 1945
"Took part in landings during North African Campaign with an Infantry unit and later served with a Special Air Unit in Italy as patrol and guard on small detachments lying-up in enemy territory. His presence with these parties saved many of them from discovery and subsequent capture or destruction. Rob made over 20 parachute descents."

Thorn – Alsatian
MAP Serving with Civil Defence
Date of Award: 2 March 1945
"For locating air-raid casualties in spite of thick smoke in a burning building."

Rifleman Khan – Alsatian
147. 6th Battalion Cameronians (SR)
Date of Award: 27 March 1945
"For rescuing L/Cpl. Muldoon from drowning under heavy shell fire at the assault of Walcheren, November 1944, while serving with the 6th Cameronians (SR)."

Rex – Alsatian
MAP Civil Defence Rescue Dog
Date of Award: April 1945
"For outstanding good work in the location of casualties in burning buildings. Undaunted by smouldering debris, thick smoke, intense heat and jets of water from fire hoses, this dog displayed uncanny intelligence and outstanding determination in his efforts to follow up any scent which led him to a trapped casualty."

Sheila – Collie
Date of Award: 2 July 1945
"For assisting in the rescue of four American Airmen lost on the Cheviots in a blizzard after an air crash in December, 1944."

Rip – Mongrel
Stray picked up by Civil Defence Squad at Poplar, London E14
Date of Award: 1945
"For locating many air-raid victims during the blitz of 1940."

Peter – Collie
Date of Award: November 1945
"For locating victims trapped under blitzed buildings while serving with the MAP attached to Civil Defence of London."

Judy – Pedigree Pointer
Date of Award: May 1946
"For magnificent courage and endurance in Japanese prison camps, which helped to maintain morale among her fellow prisoners and also for saving many lives through her intelligence and watchfulness."

Punch and Judy – Boxer dog and bitch
Date of Awards: November 1946
"These dogs saved the lives of two British Officers in Israel by attacking an armed terrorist who was stealing upon them unawares and thus warning them of their danger. Punch sustained 4 bullet wounds and Judy a long graze down her back."

Ricky – Welsh Collie
Date of Award: 29 March 1947
"This dog was engaged in cleaning the verges of the canal bank at Nederweert, Holland. He found all the mines but during the operation one of them exploded. Ricky was wounded in the head but remained calm and kept at work. Had he become excited he would have been a danger to the rest of the section working nearby."

Brian – Alsatian
Date of Award: 29 March 1947
"This patrol dog was attached to a Parachute Battalion of the 13th Battalion Airborne Division. He landed in Normandy with them and, having done the requisite number of jumps, became a fully-qualified Paratrooper."

They Also Serve

Antis – Alsatian
Date of Award: 28 January 1949
"Owned by a Czech airman, this dog served with him in the French Air Force and RAF from 1940 to 1945, both in N. Africa and England. Returning to Czechoslovakia after the war, he substantially helped his master's escape across the frontier when after the death of Jan Masaryk, he had to fly from the Communists."

Tich – Egyptian Mongrel
1st Battalion King's Royal Rifle Corps
Date of Award: 1 July 1949
"For loyalty, courage and devotion to duty under hazardous conditions of war 1941 to 1945, while serving with the 1st King's Rifle Corps in North Africa and Italy."

Gander – Newfoundland
Date of Award: awarded posthumously on 27 October 2000
"For saving the lives of Canadian infantrymen during the Battle of Lye Mun on Hong Kong Island in December 1941. On three documented occasions Gander, the Newfoundland mascot of the Royal Rifles of Canada engaged the enemy as his regiment joined the Winnipeg Grenadiers, members of Battalion Headquarters 'C' Force and other Commonwealth troops in their courageous defence of the Island. Twice Gander's attacks halted the enemy's advance and protected groups of wounded soldiers. In a final act of bravery the war dog was killed in action gathering a grenade. Without Gander's intervention many more lives would have been lost in the assault."

Appollo – German Shepherd
Date of Award: 5 March 2002
"For tireless courage in the service of humanity during the search and rescue operations in New York and Washington on and after 11 September 2001." Faithful to words of command and undaunted by the task, the dogs' work and unstinting devotion to duty stand as a testament to those lost or injured."

Salty and Roselle – Labrador Guide dogs
Date of Award: 5 March 2002
"For remaining loyally at the side of their blind owners, courageously leading them down more than 70 floors of the World Trade Center and to a place of safety following the terrorist attack on New York on 11 September 2001."

Sam – German Shepherd
Royal Army Veterinary Corps
Date of Award: 14 January 2003
"For outstanding gallantry in April 1998 while assigned to the Royal Canadian Regiment in Drvar during the conflict in Bosnia-Hertzegovina. On two documented occasions Sam displayed great courage and devotion to duty. On 18 April Sam successfully brought down an armed man threatening the lives of civilians and Service personnel. On 24 April, while guarding a compound harbouring Serbian refugees, Sam's determined approach held off rioters until reinforcements arrived. This dog's true valour saved the lives of many servicemen and civilians during this time of human conflict."

Buster – Springer Spaniel
Royal Army Veterinary Corps
Date of Award: 9 December 2003
"For outstanding gallantry in March 2003 while assigned to the Duke of Wellington's Regiment in Safwan, Southern Iraq. Arms and explosives search dog Buster located an arsenal of weapons and explosives hidden behind a false wall in a property linked with an extremist group. Buster is considered responsible for saving the lives of service personnel and civilians. Following the find, all attacks ceased and shortly afterwards and troops replaced their steel helmets with berets."

Lucky – German Shepherd
RAF number 3610 AD: RAF Police anti-terrorist tracker dog – from 1949 to 1952 during the Malaya Campaign
Date of Award: 6 February 2007
"For the outstanding gallantry and devotion to duty of the RAF Police anti-terrorist tracker dog team, comprising Bobbie, Jasper, Lassie and Lucky, while attached to the Civil Police and several British Army regiments including the Coldstream Guards, 2nd Battalion Royal Scots Guards and the Ghurkhas during the Malaya Campaign. Bobbie, Jasper, Lassie and Lucky displayed exceptional determination and life-saving skills during the Malaya Campaign. The dogs and their handlers were an exceptional team, capable of tracking and locating the enemy by scent despite unrelenting heat and an almost impregnable jungle. Sadly, three of the dogs lost their lives in the line of duty: only Lucky survived to the end of the conflict."

Sadie – Labrador
RAVC arms and explosive search dog – Kabul, Afghanistan in November 2005
Date of Award: 6 February 2007
"For outstanding gallantry and devotion to duty while assigned to the Royal Gloucestershire, Berkshire and Wiltshire Light Infantry during conflict in Afghanistan in 2005. On 14 November 2005 military personnel serving with NATO's International Security Assistance Force in Kabul were involved in two separate attacks. Sadie and Lance Corporal Yardley were deployed to search for secondary explosive devices. Sadie gave a positive indication near a concrete blast wall and multinational personnel were moved to a safe distance. Despite the obvious danger Sadie and Lance Corporal Yardley completed their search. At the site of Sadie's indication, bomb disposal operators later made safe an explosive device. The bomb was designed to inflict maximum injury. Sadie's actions undoubtedly saved the lives of many civilians and soldiers."

Treo – Labrador
Royal Army Veterinary Corps
Date of Award: 24 February 2010
"In March 2008, Treo was deployed to Helmand Province, Afghanistan, to search for weapons and munitions concealed by the Taliban. On 15 August, while acting as forward protection for 8 Platoon, The Royal Irish Regiment, Treo located an improvised explosive device on a roadside where soldiers were about to pass. On 3 and 4 September, Treo's actions detected a further device, saving 7 Platoon from guaranteed casualties. Without doubt, Treo's actions and devotion to his duties, while in the throes of conflict, saved many lives."

Theo – Springer Spaniel
Royal Army Veterinary Corps, Arms and Explosives Search dog
Date of Award: posthumously on 25 October 2012
"For outstanding gallantry and devotion to duty while deployed with 104 Military Working Dog (MWD) Squadron during conflict in Afghanistan in September 2010 to March 2011."

Sasha – Labrador
Royal Army Veterinary Corps, Arms and Explosives Search dog
Date of Award: posthumously on 21 May 2014
"For outstanding gallantry and devotion to duty while assigned to 2nd Battalion, The Parachute Regiment, in Afghanistan 2008."

PIGEONS

White Vision
Pigeon SURP.41.L.3089
Date of Award: 2 December 1943
"For delivering a message under exceptionally difficult conditions and so contributing to the rescue of an Air Crew while serving with the RAF in October 1943."

Winkie
Pigeon NEHU.40.NS.1
Date of Award: 2 December 1943
"For delivering a message under exceptionally difficult conditions and so contributing to the rescue of an Air Crew while serving with the RAF in February, 1942."

Tyke (also known as George)
Pigeon Number 1263 MEPS 43
Date of Award: 2 December 1943
"For delivering a message under exceptionally difficult conditions and so contributing to the rescue of an Air Crew, while serving with the RAF in the Mediterranean in June, 1943."

Beach Comber
Pigeon NPS.41.NS.4230
Date of Award: 6 March 1944
"For bringing the first news to this country of the landing at Dieppe, under hazardous conditions in September, 1942, while serving with the Canadian Army."

Gustav
Pigeon NPS.42.31066
Date of Award: 1 September 1944
"For delivering the first message from the Normandy Beaches from a ship off the beach-head while serving with the RAF on 6 June 1944."

Paddy
Pigeon NPS.43.9451
Date of Award: 1 September 1944
"For the best recorded time with a message from the Normandy Operations, while serving with the RAF in June, 1944."

Kenley Lass
Pigeon NURP.36.JH.190
Date of Award: March 1945
"For being the first pigeon to be used with success for secret communications from an Agent in enemy-occupied France while serving with the NPS in October 1940."

Navy Blue
Pigeon NPS.41.NS.2862
Date of Award: March 1945
"For delivering an important message from a Raiding Party on the West Coast of France, although injured, while serving with the RAF in June, 1944.

Flying Dutchman
Pigeon – NPS.42.NS.44802
Date of Award: March 1945
"For successfully delivering messages from Agents in Holland on three occasions. Missing on fourth mission, while serving with the RAF in 1944."

Dutch Coast
Pigeon NURP.41. A.2164
Date of Award: March 1945
"For delivering an SOS from a ditched Air Crew close to the enemy coast 288 miles distance in 7½ hours, under unfavourable conditions, while serving with the RAF in April 1942."

Commando
Pigeon NURP.38.EGU.242
Date of Award: March 1945
"For successfully delivering messages from Agents in Occupied France on three occasions: twice under exceptionally adverse conditions, while serving with the NPS in 1942."

Royal Blue
Pigeon NURP.40.GVIS.453
Date of award: March 1945
"For being the first pigeon in this war to deliver a message from a forced landed aircraft on the Continent while serving with the RAF in October, 1940."

Ruhr Express
Pigeon NPS.43.29018
Date of Award: May 1945
"For carrying an important message from the Ruhr Pocket in excellent time, while serving with the RAF in April, 1945."

William of Orange
Pigeon NPS.42.NS.15125
Date of Award: May 1945
"For delivering a message from the Arnhem Airborne Operation in record time for any single pigeon, while serving with the APS in September 1944."

Scotch Lass
Pigeon NPS.42.21610
Date of Award: June 1945
"For bringing 38 microphotographs across the North Sea in good time although injured, while serving with the RAF in Holland in September 1944."

Billy
Pigeon NU.41.HQ.4373
Date of Award: August 1945
"For delivering a message from a force-landed bomber, while in a state of complete collapse and under exceptionally bad weather conditions, while serving with the RAF in 1942."

Broad Arrow
Pigeon 41.BA.2793
Date of Award: October 1945
"For bringing important messages three times from enemy occupied country, viz: May 1943, June 1943 and August 1943, while serving with the Special Service from the Continent."

Pigeon NPS.42.NS.2780
Date of Award: October 1945
"For bringing important messages three times from enemy occupied country, viz: July 1942, August 1942 and April 1943, while serving with the Special Service from the Continent."

Pigeon NPS.42.NS.7524
Date of Award: October 1945
"For bringing important messages three times from enemy-occupied country, viz: July 1942, May 1943 and July 1943, while serving with the Special Service from the continent."

Maquis
Pigeon NPSNS.42.36392
Date of Award: October 1945
"For bringing important messages three times from enemy occupied country, viz: May 1943 (Amiens) February, 1944 (Combined Operations) and June, 1944 (French Maquis) while serving with the Special Service from the Continent."

Mary
Pigeon NURP.40.WCE.249
Date of Award: November 1945
"For outstanding endurance on War Service in spite of wounds."

Tommy
Pigeon NURP.41.DHZ56
Date of Award: February 1946
"For delivering a valuable message from Holland to Lancashire under difficult conditions, while serving with NPS in July 1942."

All Alone
Pigeon NURP.39.SDS.39
Date of Award: February 1946
"For delivering an important message in one day over a distance of 400 miles, while serving with the NPS in August, 1943."

Princess
Pigeon 42WD593
Date of Award: May 1946
"Sent on special mission to Crete, this pigeon returned to her loft (RAF Alexandria) having travelled about 500 miles mostly over sea, with most valuable information. One of the finest performances in the war record of the Pigeon Service."

Mercury
Pigeon NURP.37.CEN.335
Date of Award: August 1946
"For carrying out a special task involving a flight of 480 miles from Northern Denmark while serving with the Special Section Army Pigeon Service in July 1942."

Pigeon NURP.38.BPC.6.
Date of Award: August 1946
"For three outstanding flights from France while serving with the Special Section, Army Pigeon Service, 11 July 1941, 9 September 1941, and 29 November 1941."

GI Joe
Pigeon USA43SC6390
Date of Award: August 1946
"This bird is credited with making the most outstanding flight by a USA Army Pigeon in World War II. Making the 20 mile flight from British 10th Army HQ, in the same number of minutes, it brought a message which arrived just in time to save the lives of at least 100 Allied soldiers from being bombed by their own planes."

Duke of Normandy
Pigeon NURP.41.SBC.219
Date of Award: 8 January 1947
"For being the first bird to arrive with a message from Paratroops of 21st Army Group behind enemy lines on D Day 6 June, 1944, while serving with APS."

Pigeon NURP.43.CC.1418
Date of Award: 8 January 1947
"For the fastest flight with message from 6th Airborne Div. Normandy, 7 June, 1944, while serving with APS."

Pigeon DD.43.T.139 (Australian Army Signal Corps)
Date of award: February 1947

"*During a heavy tropical storm this bird was released from Army Boat 1402 which had foundered on Wadou Beach in the Huon Gulf. Homing 40 miles to Madang it brought a message which enabled a rescue ship to be sent in time to salvage the craft and its valuable cargo of stores and ammunition.*"

Pigeon DD.43.Q.879 (Australian Army Signal Corps)
Date of award: February 1947

"*During an attack by Japanese on a US Marine patrol on Manus Island, pigeons were released to warn headquarters of an impending enemy counter-attack. Two were shot down but DD43 despite heavy fire directed at it reached HQ with the result that enemy concentrations were bombed and the patrol extricated.*"

Cologne
Pigeon NURP39.NPS.144
Date of Award: unknown

"*For homing from a crashed aircraft over Cologne although seriously wounded, while serving with the RAF in 1943.*"

HORSES

Olga - Police Horse
Date of Award: 11 April 1947

"*On duty when a flying bomb demolished four houses in Tooting and a plate-glass window crashed immediately in front of her. Olga, after bolting for 100 yards, returned to the scene of the incident and remained on duty with her rider, controlling traffic and assisting rescue organisations.*"

Upstart - Police Horse
Date of Award: 11 April 1947

"*While on patrol duty in Bethnal Green a flying bomb exploded within 75 yards, showering both horse and rider with broken glass and debris. Upstart was completely unperturbed and remained quietly on duty with his rider controlling traffic, etc., until the incident had been dealt with.*"

Regal - Police Horse
Date of Award: 11 April 1947

"*Was twice in burning stables caused by explosive incendiaries at Muswell Hill. Although receiving minor injuries, being covered by debris and close to the flames, this horse showed no signs of panic.*"

CAT

Simon
Date of Award: awarded posthumously 1949
"Served on HMS Amethyst during the Yangtze Incident, disposing of many rats though wounded by shell blast. Throughout the incident his behaviour was of the highest order, although the blast was capable of making a hole over a foot in diameter in a steel plate."

HONORARY DICKIN MEDAL

The Honorary PDSA Dickin Medal was awarded in 2014 to War Horse Warrior to honour all the animals that served in the First World War. Their contribution to the Great War predates the institution of the PDSA Dickin Medal and the Honorary PDSA Dickin Medal is a unique award designed to recognise the role that ALL animals played during this time.

Appendix 2

FURTHER READING

Animals in War *by Jilly Cooper*

The Animals' War:
Animals in Wartime from the First World War to the Present Day
by Juliet Gardiner/Imperial War Museum

The Animals' VC: For Gallantry or Devotion: The PDSA Dickin Medal
by David Long

The Animal Victoria Cross *by Peter Hawthorne*

Animal Heroes *by David Long*

Tommy's Ark: Soldiers and Their Animals in the Great War
by Richard Van Emden

The War Horses *by Simon Butler*

Warrior *by Isabel George*

The Dog that Saved my Life *by Isabel George*

It's All About Treo *by David Heyhoe*

Antis:
    One Man and His Dog *by Anthony Richardson*
    War Dog *by Damien Lewis*
    The Dog who could Fly *by Damien Lewis*
    Freedom in the Air *by Hamish Ross*

Judy:
    Judy VC *by E Varley*
    Prisoner of War: Judy *by Isabel George*
    Judy: A Dog in a Million *by Damien Lewis*
    No Better Friend *by Robert Weintraub*

Simon:
    Simon Ships Out *by Jacky Donovan*
    www.Purr-n-fur.org.uk

They Also Serve

Many and various animals were employed to support British and Allied Forces in wars and campaigns over the centuries, and as a result millions died. From the pigeon to the elephant, they all played a vital role in every region of the world in the cause of human freedom.
Their contribution must never be forgotten.

*– inscription on the Animals in War Memorial,
Hyde Park, London*

ABOUT THE AUTHOR

Rosemary Greenlaw has had a life-long passion for animals, and currently has two small but very demanding rehomed dogs. She was raised as an Air Force brat, and her interest in things military came together with her love of animals to produce this book. She lives in the Highlands of Scotland.

Cover image © Rosemary Greenlaw

Printed in Great Britain
by Amazon